Digital Deception

How Public Access and False
MFA Broke the Internet

Christopher Murphy

Apress®

Digital Deception: How Public Access and False MFA Broke the Internet

Christopher Murphy
Clearwater, FL, USA

ISBN-13 (pbk): 979-8-8688-1226-2   ISBN-13 (electronic): 979-8-8688-1227-9
https://doi.org/10.1007/979-8-8688-1227-9

Managing Director, Apress Media LLC: Welmoed Spahr
Acquisitions Editor: Susan McDermott
Development Editor: Laura Berendson
Project Manager: Jessica Vakili

Distributed to the book trade worldwide by Springer Science+Business Media New York, 1 New York Plaza, New York, NY 10004. Phone 1-800-SPRINGER, fax (201) 348-4505, e-mail orders-ny@springer-sbm.com, or visit www.springeronline.com. Apress Media, LLC is a California LLC and the sole member (owner) is Springer Science + Business Media Finance Inc (SSBM Finance Inc). SSBM Finance Inc is a **Delaware** corporation.

For information on translations, please e-mail booktranslations@springernature.com; for reprint, paperback, or audio rights, please e-mail bookpermissions@springernature.com.

Apress titles may be purchased in bulk for academic, corporate, or promotional use. eBook versions and licenses are also available for most titles. For more information, reference our Print and eBook Bulk Sales web page at http://www.apress.com/bulk-sales.

If disposing of this product, please recycle the paper

To my wife, my business partner, and my true editor: none of the thoughts that swirl in my mind would have ever reached the page without your dedication and patience. You took my dyslexic scribbles and transformed them into words that resonate. I love you, and I am forever grateful to you for making this book possible.

To my children, who stood steadfast by my side through my darkest hours: thank you for your unwavering support and belief in me.

To my circle of friends, a rare and invaluable few, who acted with integrity and stood firm when the world sought to stifle a revolutionizing solution to the cyber crisis before it could take root: thank you Therese, Terri, Patty, Philip, Darlene, and Michael. Your encouragement, prayers, and steadfast presence have meant more than words can express. I am forever grateful for your unwavering support and loyalty.

Table of Contents

About the Author

Chris Murphy is a cybersecurity expert and pioneer in digital identity and secure network interaction. With over 25 years of experience in the field, Chris has worked with private organizations and government agencies, developing innovative solutions to eliminate vulnerabilities in network security. He is the inventor of EAID technology, a groundbreaking approach to direct user interaction, and has dedicated his career to addressing cybersecurity's most persistent challenges. This book is his effort to share these insights with a broader audience and offer actionable solutions to a broken system.

Letter from the Author

Dear Reader,

My purpose in this book is simple: to present the facts as they are. In a world where the truth can sometimes deviate from reality, both truth and reality suffer as a result. History, too, is uncompromising, it simply *is*, and the judgment of history can be both unsettling and harsh. My goal in writing this book is not to offend or accuse but to enlighten, to offer a clear and factual path out of the darkness of deception that has clouded the cybersecurity landscape for far too long.

Throughout these pages, I will highlight strategic moments where actions could and should have been taken, moments that would have altered the course of cybersecurity as we know it. The facts presented here are not malleable; they are binary in nature, and they exist independent of how anyone might feel about them. If you find yourself offended by what you read, it may be because the truth hits a bit too close to home. Yet, this does not change the facts.

This book is what it is, and the facts are what they are. My intention is to shine a light on the realities of our cybersecurity past and present, not to pass judgment or assign blame. The responsibility lies with each of us to interpret these facts with an open mind and to recognize the opportunities we have moving forward by addressing the mistakes of the past.

Thank you for taking the time to engage with this material. My hope is that by the end, you will see the same clear path forward that I do, a path that leads away from deception and toward a future where security is grounded in undeniable truths.

Sincerely,
Chris

Preface

In the rapidly evolving world of cybersecurity, we find ourselves at a critical juncture, a moment in time where the decisions we make today will shape the future of our digital lives for generations to come. Yet, despite the constant advancements in technology, a fundamental truth remains: our security is only as strong as the foundations upon which it is built.

This book, *Digital Deception*, is an exploration of those foundations and an unflinching look at how they have been compromised over time. It is a journey through the history of cybersecurity, tracing the decisions, both intentional and negligent, that have brought us to the current state of crisis. In these pages, you will discover how short-term thinking, driven by convenience and profit, has led to long-term vulnerabilities that threaten not only our privacy but the very fabric of our digital society.

This book is not just retrospective. It is also a call to action, a road map for reclaiming the integrity of our networks and our identities. Through a detailed examination of the flaws in current security practices, this book will guide you to an understanding of where we went wrong and, more importantly, how we can course correct. The facts laid out here are not meant to provoke fear or anger but to inspire change.

As you delve into this book, you will encounter truths that may be uncomfortable, even unsettling. But it is only by facing these truths head-on that we can begin to address the deep-seated issues within the cybersecurity industry. This is not a book for those who prefer to look the other way or for those who are content with the status quo. It is a book for those who are ready to challenge conventional wisdom, to question the systems we've come to rely on, and to demand better.

The path ahead is not an easy one, but it is a necessary one. If we are to secure the future of the Internet and protect the countless individuals who rely on it, we must confront the failures of the past with clear eyes and a steadfast commitment to doing what is right. This book offers the facts, the context, and the guidance needed to embark on that journey.

Welcome to *Digital Deception*. Let us begin the work of setting things right.

CHAPTER 1

The Myth of Mitigation

For decades, the cybersecurity industry has been built on a myth, a belief that computer errors can be managed rather than corrected. This approach has given rise to a multibillion-dollar mitigation industry, where layers of security are stacked upon one another in the hopes of keeping attackers at bay. However, the truth is far more unsettling: no amount of mitigation can truly secure a system that is fundamentally flawed.

Mitigation, at its core, is about damage control. It acknowledges that vulnerabilities exist but seeks to minimize their impact through various security measures. Firewalls, intrusion detection systems, and encryption protocols are all part of this approach, each designed to address specific weaknesses within a network. But these solutions, while effective in the short term, do little to address the root cause of insecurity.

The rise of mitigation can be traced back to the early days of the Internet when the decision was made to prioritize public access over security. The Internet's creators did not foresee the scale at which their invention would grow nor the myriad threats that would emerge as a result. Security was an afterthought, and the vulnerabilities that were baked into the system have persisted ever since.

The Consequences of Public Access

One of the most significant consequences of this decision has been the reliance on transmitted data for authentication. Single-Factor Authentication (SFA) systems, which rely on something the user knows (like a password), have become the standard for securing online accounts.

© Christopher Murphy 2025
C. Murphy, *Digital Deception*, Apress Pocket Guides,
https://doi.org/10.1007/979-8-8688-1227-9_1

But passwords are inherently weak, easily guessed, stolen, or hacked. To compensate for this weakness, the industry introduced Multi-Factor Authentication (MFA), which was intended to add an additional layer of security by requiring something the user has (like a token) or something the user is (like a fingerprint).

The Flaws in Multi-Factor Authentication

However, the implementation of MFA has been deeply flawed. Instead of requiring multiple distinct factors, so-called MFA systems merely add layers of SFA, relying on transmitted data to authenticate users. This approach does not meet the true definition of MFA, which requires more than one distinct factor to verify identity. As a result, these systems remain vulnerable to the same attacks that plague SFA without all the layers of mitigation.

The Illusion of Security Layers

The proliferation of mitigation solutions has only compounded the problem. Each new security product adds another layer of complexity to a system, increasing the likelihood of misconfiguration and creating new opportunities for attackers. In a 2019 survey, 53% of enterprises admitted that they had no idea if their security tools are working effectively. This staggering figure highlights the inefficacy of the current approach to cybersecurity and the false sense of security it provides.

The Cost of Mitigation

Moreover, the cost of maintaining these complex security stacks is enormous. Organizations spend billions of dollars each year on mitigation products, yet breaches continue to occur with alarming frequency. This raises an uncomfortable question: If mitigation is not working, why does the industry continue to rely on it?

The Role of Economic Incentives

The answer may lie in the economic incentives that drive the cybersecurity industry. Vendors profit from selling mitigation solutions, and organizations are willing to pay for them because they believe they are necessary to protect their networks. But this belief is based on a flawed premise, that vulnerabilities can be managed rather than eliminated.

A Shift Toward Eliminating Vulnerabilities

To break free from the cycle of mitigation, the industry must shift its focus from managing vulnerabilities to eliminating them. This requires a fundamental change in the way we think about security. Instead of relying on public access models and transmitted data, we must adopt a private access model that provides genuine MFA.

Digital IDs: A Path to Real Security

The introduction of digital IDs and direct user interaction is the key to achieving this goal. Digital IDs provide a secure means of verifying identity, eliminating the reliance on passwords and other transmitted data. By requiring users to interact directly with the system, a private access model removes the vulnerabilities associated with public logins and makes it virtually impossible for attackers to gain unauthorized access.

The Future of Cybersecurity

The transition to a private access model will not be easy, but it is necessary if we are to achieve true security. It will require organizations to rethink their approach to cybersecurity, moving away from the myth of mitigation and embracing the reality that vulnerabilities can be eliminated. It will also require vendors to develop new products that focus on security by design rather than security through layers.

Simplicity As the Solution

The future of cybersecurity lies in simplicity. By eliminating the need for mitigation, we can create systems that are inherently secure, reducing the attack surface and making it more difficult for attackers to succeed. This is not a distant vision; it is a practical solution that can be implemented today.

Conclusion: The End of Mitigation

The time for mitigation has passed. The path forward is clear: adopt a private access model, implement genuine MFA, and eliminate the vulnerabilities that have plagued the network security since its inception. Only then can we achieve the true security that has long eluded us.

CHAPTER 2

Public Access: The Original Flaw

The Critical Decision

The cybersecurity crisis we face today can be traced back to a single, fundamental decision: allowing public access to secure networks. This chapter explores how the decision to implement public access models, beginning with the first so-called "secure public portals," introduced vulnerabilities that have since compounded and spread across the entire digital landscape. While the Internet was initially built for openness, the decision to extend public access to secure environments created an inherent flaw, one that has multiplied over time, resulting in today's widespread cybersecurity breaches.

The Early Days: Necessity over Security

In the early days of the Internet, public access was a necessity. The Internet was a tool for open communication, research, and collaboration. Public access to information was its foundation, and this openness allowed it to

© Christopher Murphy 2025
C. Murphy, *Digital Deception*, Apress Pocket Guides,
https://doi.org/10.1007/979-8-8688-1227-9_2

expand rapidly. However, when secure networks (handling sensitive data, financial transactions, and government records) were connected to the public-facing World Wide Web (WWW), a critical flaw was introduced.

Transmitted Data: A Weak Foundation

Rather than creating a private access model that would restrict entry to only authorized users, the industry chose to rely on public access login pages, using transmitted data (such as passwords and other credentials) to authenticate users. This decision, which seemed practical at the time, opened the door to unauthorized users and eventually cybercriminals, allowing them to access secure systems with nothing more than a guess. It also created a system where the identity of users could only be guessed and verified through data transmission, exposing every system to interception, manipulation, and theft.

A Growing Problem

This decision was made during a time when the scope of the Internet was still relatively small, and the risks were not fully understood. However, as the Internet grew and the number of users exploded, the vulnerabilities in this model became glaringly obvious. Despite these growing risks, the decision to retain public logins to secure networks was never seriously reconsidered. Instead of closing access and moving to private models, the industry doubled down on mitigation solutions to try to patch over the weaknesses inherent in the public access model.

Binary Security Principles

The introduction of public access models fundamentally violated the core principles of security protocols, which are designed to ensure that only authorized individuals can access secure environments. Security protocols, when properly implemented, are binary: either a system is secure, or it is not. The decision to rely on public access introduced an inherent weakness that could never be fully secured because it relied on guessing identity rather than verifiable interaction.

The Cybercriminal's Entry Point

Every public access portal, every login page, every publicly accessible system created an entry point for cybercriminals. These login pages allowed anyone with Internet access to submit credentials and attempt to access the system. Even with multiple layers of authentication or mitigation, the very existence of a public-facing login undermined the security of the entire system. Every attempt to secure these systems became a Band-Aid solution, layering complexity on top of a core vulnerability that could never be truly resolved as long as public access remained part of the model.

The Role of Transmitted Data

The reliance on transmitted data for identity verification compounded the problem. Transmitted data, whether in the form of passwords, tokens, or biometric signatures, can be intercepted, manipulated, or spoofed. The decision to allow public access meant that all security systems were forced to rely on data traveling through insecure, public networks, rather than establishing a direct, secure interaction between the user and the system.

Piling on Layers

Once public access became the norm, every subsequent security measure was built on top of this flawed foundation. Rather than addressing the root cause, public exposure, organizations continued to add mitigation solutions to patch the growing vulnerabilities. Each new layer of mitigation added complexity to the system, but it did not eliminate the original flaw: the open public access points.

A Crime Scene of Complexity

Every mitigation strategy compounded the problem, making systems more complex and harder to secure. The more layers that were added, the more points of failure were introduced, and the more exploitable the system became. What started as a practical decision in the early days of the Internet evolved into a complex and fragile system, where security was dependent on an ever-growing stack of patches rather than addressing the core vulnerability.

The Private Access Solution

The solution to this problem has always been private access, a model where only authorized users can interact with the system and where there is no public-facing login for cybercriminals to exploit. In a private access model, users must possess something physical (such as a digital identification) that grants them entry to the system. This eliminates the need for public login pages and removes the guessing of identity.

A Missed Opportunity

With private access, there is no need to rely on transmitted data for authentication because the user interacts directly with the system using a physical digital ID. This ensures that only authorized individuals can access the network and makes it impossible for cybercriminals to attempt to breach the system from a distance.

Conclusion: Closing the Public Access Doors

Had the industry embraced private access from the beginning, the entire cybercrime landscape would look very different today. Instead of relying on mitigation, organizations would have built their systems with real security at the core, and the vulnerabilities introduced by public access would never have existed.

The decision to implement public access to secure networks was the original flaw that set the stage for today's cybersecurity crisis. By opening secure networks to public-facing logins, the industry created a system that was inherently insecure and could never be fully protected. Every subsequent security measure has been an attempt to patch this core flaw, but as long as public access remains part of the model, true security cannot be achieved.

By embracing private access, the vulnerabilities that have plagued the network security for decades can be eliminated. The choice to grant public access may have been made from necessity, but continuing down this path is no longer tenable. The time for real security is now, and it begins with closing the public access doors.

CHAPTER 3

The Legal and Economic Time Bomb of MFA Deception

The Fatal Flaw in Public Access

The decision to grant public access to secure networks made genuine Multi-Factor Authentication (MFA) impossible. MFA, by definition, requires users to possess something tangible, like a digital ID, to confirm their identity alongside something they know, such as a password. However, when public logins were introduced, this critical "have" factor was replaced by Single-Factor Authentication (SFA), which relied solely on transmitted data to guess identity, undermining the entire MFA security model. What was intended to be a revolution in digital security quickly became a global deception.

© Christopher Murphy 2025
C. Murphy, *Digital Deception*, Apress Pocket Guides,
https://doi.org/10.1007/979-8-8688-1227-9_3

The Three Factors of Genuine MFA

The essence of genuine MFA lies in three distinct factors:

1. **Something the User Has**: A tangible item, such as a digital ID

2. **Something the User Is**: Their physical presence or connection to the system

3. **Something the User Knows**: Credentials like a password, PIN, or biometrics

The introduction of public access models collapsed the foundation of this structure, as organizations began relying on public logins and transmitted data. Without requiring a tangible, physical presence, such as a digital ID, genuine MFA became impossible, leading to the widespread adoption of SFA disguised as MFA. This decision to prioritize convenience and expediency over real security has opened networks to unprecedented levels of risk and created a ticking time bomb for organizations that falsely claim MFA compliance.

Regulatory Warnings Ignored

In 2001, the Federal Financial Institutions Examination Council (FFIEC) introduced MFA regulations aimed at shifting security away from reliance on transmitted data and toward a private access model, where user identity would be confirmed through physical interaction with a digital ID. However, the industry rejected this approach. Instead of adopting the private access model necessary for real security, organizations continued to rely on public logins and SFA while falsely claiming MFA compliance.

By 2006, the FFIEC issued a directive clarifying that true MFA, as defined, required more than transmitted data. However, the industry ignored this call for genuine security and continued to promote the illusion of compliance. Other regulatory bodies, such as the National Institute of Standards and Technology (NIST) and the European Union, followed suit, creating frameworks that allowed public access models to masquerade as MFA-compliant systems. This deception was driven by short-term economic incentives, as companies found it more convenient and profitable to sell and adopt false solutions than to overhaul their security models.

The Cybersecurity Environment Built on a Lie

The global reliance on public access and transmitted data created a cybersecurity environment built on a lie. Organizations claimed to comply with MFA standards while continuing to operate systems based on SFA. The result is an entire industry mired in false security claims, where real MFA has never been implemented and public access models remain the norm.

The Legal and Financial Implications

The decision to perpetuate the MFA deception has profound legal and financial implications. The introduction of public logins and the reliance on transmitted data have made networks inherently vulnerable, and as the truth about the MFA deception comes to light, the legal and financial consequences are becoming inescapable.

Organizations that have falsely claimed MFA compliance have left themselves open and exposed to significant legal liabilities. As more breaches occur, regulators, consumers, and plaintiffs' attorneys will have an easier time proving that companies either knowingly relied on inadequate security measures or trusted "experts" that misinformed them of the reality of the products being purchased. Every breach that occurs under the guise of false compliance increases the risk of lawsuits, regulatory fines, and class-action cases, creating massive legal exposure for these organizations.

The Staggering Economic Cost

Regulatory bodies, like the FFIEC, NIST, and the European Union, have begun to face increasing pressure to enforce compliance with genuine MFA standards. The economic cost of this failure is staggering. Cybercrime is already causing over $10 trillion in damages annually, and this figure is projected to double in the coming years. The global economy is bearing the weight of an industry built on deceptive security claims. The decision to prioritize mitigation over correction has not only left networks exposed but also passed the financial burden of cyberattacks onto organizations and users alike.

The Illusion of Mitigation

Rather than adopting a private access model and issuing digital IDs to authorized users, organizations have turned to mitigation solutions to create the illusion of security. These mitigation strategies, layer upon layer of patches and workarounds, do not meet the binary requirements of genuine MFA. Instead of addressing the root cause of insecurity (public access models), they only attempt to manage the risk, allowing vulnerabilities to persist beneath the surface.

The False Sense of Security

This approach has created a false sense of security across industries. Many companies believe that by adding more security layers, they are adequately protecting themselves from threats. But every new breach reveals the cracks in this approach, as cybercriminals continue to exploit the system's underlying vulnerabilities. The reliance on mitigation solutions has perpetuated the myth that complexity can provide security, when in reality, it has only made systems more fragile and prone to exploitation.

The Cost of Inaction

The failure to adopt genuine MFA has left the entire cybersecurity industry vulnerable to cyberattacks as well as the legal fallout from falsified compliance. With over $24.8 trillion in damages already caused by cybercrime in the last five years, the cost of inaction is staggering. Organizations are spending billions on mitigation solutions that do nothing to solve the core problem, creating an unsustainable cycle of patching vulnerabilities rather than eliminating them.

The Impact on Consumers

The cost of breaches is not limited to the organizations themselves. As companies continue to fail in securing their systems, they pass the financial burden onto consumers in the form of higher prices, increased fees, and lost trust. The real victims of the MFA deception are the users whose data is exposed, their identities compromised, and their financial security undermined.

The Time Bomb Is Ticking

The global reliance on public login models has created an economic time bomb. As more breaches occur and more legal challenges are filed, the financial burden will become unsustainable. Every day of delay only adds to the mounting costs. The global economy cannot continue to absorb the damage caused by an industry built on false claims of security.

The Path Forward: Genuine MFA

To avoid the inevitable legal and financial fallout, organizations must act now. The solution is simple: adopt a private access model and implement genuine MFA based on direct user interaction with a digital ID. By eliminating public access and transmitted data, organizations can finally provide the level of security required by regulatory frameworks.

The Reckoning for Public Access Models

Every claim of MFA compliance under current public login models is untrue. No amount of mitigation can change the fact that public access models are, by definition, SFA, not MFA. The only way to meet the standards set by the FFIEC, NIST, and other regulatory bodies is to implement a private access model where user identity is verified through direct interaction with a physical digital ID.

Conclusion: The End of MFA Deception

Organizations that continue to rely on public access models are at risk of legal collapse. The reckoning is inevitable. Legal challenges are mounting, and as the truth about MFA deception comes to light, the consequences will be swift and severe. The time for mitigation first has passed.
Private access and genuine MFA must become the standard to protect corporate and government assets as well as the global economy from further damage.

CHAPTER 4

The Pervasiveness of Cybersecurity Deception

Cybersecurity deception has become a defining characteristic of the digital age, with its reach extending far beyond isolated breaches or system failures. Today, this deception is pervasive, woven into the very fabric of how networks are protected, how products are sold, and how security is marketed. As companies continue to rely on flawed systems and falsified compliance, the ripple effects spread across industries, leaving a trail of damage, deception, and unmet regulatory requirements.

The Deceptive Nature of Cybersecurity Products

At the center of the problem is the deceptive representation of cybersecurity products marketed and sold as effective solutions to the growing threat of cybercrime. Many companies that develop and sell these products market them as comprehensive security measures, but they are built on outdated and flawed assumptions. For instance, vendors continue

© Christopher Murphy 2025
C. Murphy, *Digital Deception*, Apress Pocket Guides,
https://doi.org/10.1007/979-8-8688-1227-9_4

to sell MFA solutions that rely on transmitted data and public access models, despite knowing that these solutions fail to meet the standards for genuine MFA.

These vendors are not just misleading their customers; they are actively contributing to the proliferation of cybercrime. By selling mitigation solutions that patch over vulnerabilities without addressing the core security flaw, they create a false sense of security for organizations while leaving them exposed to breaches. In essence, the industry has normalized the sale of insecure products, making deception part of the business model.

False Compliance with Regulatory Standards

Even worse, many vendors market their products as compliant with regulatory standards, including MFA regulations. These claims of compliance are rarely scrutinized, allowing vendors to continue selling SFA disguised as MFA to organizations that believe they are securing their systems. This systemic deception has spread across industries, as organizations rely on the assurances of vendors and fail to verify whether the solutions they are implementing meet binary security principles.

The continued reliance on public access models is another example of the pervasive deception within the cybersecurity industry. Public access models expose networks to guessing identity, yet they remain the default approach for securing systems. By allowing anyone to attempt to log in via a public-facing portal, these models create a massive attack surface that cybercriminals are exploiting.

The Inherent Weakness of Public Access

Organizations that rely on public access models claim that they are following best practices by layering on additional security measures like MFA. However, because these security measures are built on top of a public access foundation, they are already inherently flawed. No matter how many mitigation layers are added, the system will always be vulnerable because the core weakness remains: public access opens the door to unauthorized users.

This approach has created an industry-wide belief that public access is an acceptable trade-off if mitigation strategies are in place. But this belief is based on false security, perpetuating the idea that systems are secure when in fact they are not. The reality is that if public access logins exist, the system is fundamentally insecure, and the use of alleged MFA or other security measures cannot alter that fact.

The Role of Regulators in Cybersecurity Deception

Regulators are supposed to be the gatekeepers of security standards, ensuring that organizations meet the requirements set by MFA regulations and other security frameworks. However, regulators have failed to enforce compliance, allowing falsified MFA claims to proliferate. This lack of oversight has contributed to the widespread deception within the industry, as organizations feel emboldened to continue claiming compliance without meeting the actual standards.

For example, the introduction of the FFIEC's 2006 "By definition true MFA" was supposed to set a new standard for Multi-Factor Authentication, requiring that distinct factors, such as something the user has, something the user is, and something the user knows, be used to verify identity. Yet, since its introduction, regulatory enforcement of this standard has been nonexistent. Many organizations claim to be MFA compliant, when in reality, they continue to rely on SFA solutions that do not meet the criteria outlined by the regulation.

The Culture of Complacency

This failure to enforce compliance has created a culture of complacency within organizations, where security standards are treated as aspirational goals that need never be achieved rather than mandatory requirements. Without strict regulatory oversight, organizations are free to implement inadequate security measures and continue making false claims of compliance. The result is a system where falsified security is not just common, it's the norm.

The complicity of the entire cybersecurity industry in this widespread deception is undeniable. Vendors, regulators, and organizations have all contributed to an environment where security products are sold, implemented, and marketed based on false claims. Each actor plays a role in perpetuating the deception:

- Vendors profit from selling mitigation solutions that patch vulnerabilities without solving the core issue.

- Organizations implement these solutions, claiming compliance with regulations, without verifying the effectiveness of the products they are using.

- Regulators fail to audit or enforce the real compliance necessary to protect systems from cybercriminals.

The Consequences for Consumers

This collective complicity has created a perfect storm of cybersecurity deception, where insecurity is built into the very systems that are supposed to protect users. Every breach, every instance of falsified compliance, and every product sold based on misrepresentation adds another layer of deception to the system. The result is a digital economy that is built on false promises, one where trust has been eroded and security is an illusion.

At the heart of this deception are the consumers; the individuals and businesses that trust experts and cybersecurity solutions to protect their sensitive data. Each time a product is sold based on falsified claims of security, it is the users who suffer the consequences. Breaches expose their personal information, and they are left to bear the financial costs of identity theft, fraudulent transactions, and lost privacy.

What's more, the economic burden of cybercrime is often passed on to consumers in the form of higher prices, increased fees, and hidden costs. Organizations that fail to protect their networks raise their prices to cover the costs of cyber breaches, passing the financial damage onto their customers. Consumers, who trust that the systems they interact with are secure, end up paying the price for systems built on deception that are damaging them.

A Call for Accountability

The pervasiveness of cybersecurity deception highlights the need for accountability at every level of the industry. Vendors must stop selling insecure products based on false claims of compliance. Organizations must stop relying on insecure public access models and transmitted data and begin implementing a private access model that provides genuine MFA. Regulators must enforce the security standards that have already been established and audit organizations to ensure they are truly compliant.

The only way to stop the cycle of deception is to embrace real security, security that is built on binary principles, where the decisions made are either secure or not. Private access, combined with digital IDs, eliminates the need for public-facing portals and introduces a binary truth into the authentication process. This is the only path to restoring trust in the cybersecurity industry and protecting the global economy from the escalating costs of cybercrime.

Conclusion: Ending Cybersecurity Deception

The cybersecurity industry has become a system built on deception, where falsified compliance and misrepresentation are accepted as part of doing business. This pervasive deception affects every aspect of the digital economy, from the products sold to the regulatory standards that are supposed to protect users.

Without accountability and a commitment to real security, the problem will only get worse. Organizations, vendors, and regulators must confront the deception at the heart of the industry and take steps to implement real solutions based on binary security principles. The time for falsified compliance is over, and the future must be built on truth.

CHAPTER 5

Complicity Through Blind Conformity

The cybersecurity industry is not just grappling with technological flaws and systemic deception; it is also suffering from the dangerous effects of blind conformity. A culture has emerged where questioning flawed security models is seen as unnecessary or even detrimental to career growth. Professionals within the industry, whether they are security experts, executives, or regulators, are often pressured to accept established practices without considering their validity or efficacy. This blind conformity has led to complicity in the ongoing deception that defines today's cybersecurity.

The Failure to Embrace Nonconformity

At the heart of this complicity lies the failure to embrace nonconformity as a pathway to improvement. To quote Ralph Waldo Emerson in his seminal essay "Self-Reliance": "Speak what you think now in hard words, and tomorrow speak what tomorrow thinks in hard words again, though it contradict everything you said today." This philosophy should be the guiding light for every cybersecurity expert. The simple act of learning, of recognizing a flaw and taking action to correct it, remains the solution to the industry's crisis. Yet, the pressures of blind conformity have kept professionals from embracing this approach, leading to the perpetuation of errors and the erosion of security.

© Christopher Murphy 2025
C. Murphy, *Digital Deception*, Apress Pocket Guides,
https://doi.org/10.1007/979-8-8688-1227-9_5

Established Practices and Their Flaws

The tendency to conform without question has allowed many of the systemic issues within the cybersecurity industry to go unchecked. Professionals in the field are often taught to rely on established security practices and solutions, even when those solutions are known to be flawed. The assumption is that if a model is widely adopted and supported by vendors and regulators, it must be valid. However, this mindset overlooks the reality that many of these practices were built on outdated assumptions that no longer apply to the modern threat landscape.

The Fear of Standing Out

This dynamic is further complicated by the fact that many experts within the industry have built their careers on the very systems and practices that are now under scrutiny. Admitting that these models are flawed would require acknowledging that decades of hard work have been built on faulty assumptions, a reality that many are unwilling to face. As a result, the industry continues to perpetuate practices that do not provide real security, while professionals remain complicit through their refusal to question the status quo.

The pressure to conform is not just a product of technical ignorance, it is also a result of the social dynamics within the cybersecurity industry. Experts who challenge established practices or suggest alternative models are often met with resistance or ridicule. There is a deep-seated fear of standing out from the crowd, as doing so can lead to being labeled as a troublemaker or nonconformist. This fear discourages professionals from raising valid concerns about the integrity of the systems they are asked to support.

Silencing Dissent

Emerson's words resonate here: "To believe your own thought, to believe that what is true for you in your private heart is true for all men, that is genius." The challenge for professionals is to embrace their own understanding of security protocols, even when it contradicts the widely accepted practices of the industry. Yet, the social pressures within cybersecurity often prevent individuals from doing so. Those who speak out against flawed systems are dismissed as eccentric or even delusional, even though their insights are grounded in the binary logic of security.

For instance, when experts point out that so-called MFA solutions are actually Single-Factor Authentication (SFA) in disguise, they are often met with condescending remarks like, "You are the only person who believes this science, maybe you are wrong". This attitude effectively silences dissent, pushing those who are aware of the deception to either conform or risk their professional reputation.

Complicity Through Education and Certification

Blind conformity is not just a social issue, it is a cycle that perpetuates complicity in cybersecurity deception. Each time a professional accepts an insecure model without questioning it, they are contributing to the broader deception that defines today's cybersecurity environment. This complicity extends to vendors, who continue to sell mitigation solutions that they *know* do not provide real security, and to regulators, who fail to enforce true compliance with standards they established and published.

The cycle of complicity is also reinforced by the education system, where cybersecurity professionals are often taught to focus on product configuration rather than the underlying science of security protocols. Many of these education programs are funded or supported by corporations with a vested interest in maintaining the status quo, further discouraging professionals from challenging the validity of the systems they are trained to implement.

The Limitations of Certification Programs

This lack of critical thinking extends to the certification programs that cybersecurity professionals are required to complete. Many of these programs are built around specific products or systems, teaching professionals how to configure these tools without encouraging them to question whether the tools themselves are built on sound security principles. As a result, professionals enter the field with preconceived notions about what constitutes effective security, and they are unlikely to challenge these notions once they are embedded in their daily work.

Stifling Innovation

The tendency to conform without question has stifled innovation and progress within the cybersecurity industry. Rather than seeking out new and more effective ways to secure networks, professionals are content to rely on existing solutions, even when those solutions are known to be flawed. This unwillingness to challenge the status quo has created an environment where real security is sacrificed in favor of convenience and complacency.

A Call to Professional Responsibility

At its core, this problem is one of professional responsibility. Cybersecurity professionals have an obligation to ensure that the systems they build and support are secure. Yet, the pressure to conform often leads them to compromise their integrity in favor of career advancement or professional acceptance. The result is a cybersecurity industry that is more focused on maintaining appearances than on delivering real protection to its users.

Breaking the Cycle

The only way to break the cycle of blind conformity and complicity is to encourage critical thinking within the cybersecurity industry. Professionals must be willing to challenge established practices, question the validity of widely accepted models, and demand real solutions that provide genuine security.

This shift will require a fundamental change in the way cybersecurity professionals are educated, trained, and certified. Education programs must focus on teaching the binary logic of security protocols rather than simply training professionals to configure products. Certification programs must prioritize critical analysis and problem-solving over product knowledge, ensuring that professionals are equipped to make informed decisions about the security systems they implement.

Fostering Critical Thinking

Additionally, there must be a cultural shift within the industry that encourages openness to new ideas and critical inquiry. Professionals should be empowered to question the validity of the systems they work with, without fear of being ostracized or ridiculed. As Emerson argued, "Is it so bad, then, to be misunderstood?... To be great is to be misunderstood." By fostering an environment of intellectual honesty and critical thinking, the cybersecurity industry can begin to move away from the culture of blind conformity and toward a future where real security is prioritized.

Conclusion: Toward a Secure Future

The culture of blind conformity has led to widespread complicity in the ongoing cybersecurity deception that defines the industry today. By failing to question flawed systems and accepting false claims of security, professionals across the industry have contributed to a crisis that threatens the very foundation of the digital economy.

Breaking this cycle will require a commitment to critical thinking and professional integrity. Cybersecurity professionals must be willing to challenge the systems they are asked to support, demand real solutions, and reject the pressure to conform to outdated and insecure models. As Emerson's hard words remind us, learning from our mistakes and acting is the true solution. The future of cybersecurity depends on it.

CHAPTER 6

The Failure of the Cybersecurity Education System

One of the most significant failures of the cybersecurity education system is its emphasis on product configuration over the science of security protocols. Many educational programs, particularly those tied to certifications, teach students how to configure and deploy specific cybersecurity tools without ever addressing the underlying principles that govern network security. This focus on technical skills rather than scientific understanding produces professionals who can follow instructions but lack the ability to think critically about whether the solutions they are implementing are truly secure.

The Problem with Vendor-Driven Training

As a result, cybersecurity professionals are trained to view security through the lens of vendor products rather than the binary nature of security decisions. This creates a dangerous dynamic where professionals become more concerned with ensuring that their products are configured correctly than with evaluating whether those products provide the security needed to protect a network. This misguided focus has allowed flawed security models, such as public access MFA, to proliferate unchecked.

© Christopher Murphy 2025
C. Murphy, *Digital Deception*, Apress Pocket Guides,
https://doi.org/10.1007/979-8-8688-1227-9_6

The Failure to Teach Binary Security Principles

The failure to teach the binary nature of security decisions, where every choice is either secure or insecure, is perhaps the greatest oversight of the cybersecurity education system. Binary science is the foundation of all computer operations, and it is the key to understanding why certain security protocols work while others do not. Yet, many professionals graduate without ever learning that order of action, logical progression, and cause and effect are the bedrock of cybersecurity. Instead, they are taught to implement pre-built solutions, leaving them ill-equipped to solve complex problems when those solutions fail.

Corporate Influence on Education

One reason for this failure is the corporate influence on cybersecurity education. Many educational programs and certifications are sponsored or directly influenced by cybersecurity vendors, who have a vested interest in promoting the use of their products. As a result, curricula are often tailored to teach students how to configure and deploy specific tools rather than encouraging them to think critically about whether those tools are the best solution for a given problem.

This focus on vendor-driven education creates a pipeline where students are taught to rely on existing security solutions rather than developing their own approaches. It also perpetuates the idea that convenience and efficiency are more important than security, as many of the tools being promoted prioritize ease of use over real protection.

Loyalty to Products over Security

The influence of corporations in cybersecurity education is not inherently negative; many tools developed by vendors play an essential role in network security. However, the overreliance on vendor-backed curricula has created a generation of professionals who are more loyal to products than to security protocols. This loyalty to products undermines the ability of professionals to challenge flawed systems or demand better solutions when they encounter insecure models in the workplace.

The Misapplication of Multi-Factor Authentication (MFA)

The failure to properly teach the principles of Multi-Factor Authentication (MFA) is one of the most glaring examples of the shortcomings of the cybersecurity education system. Many programs teach MFA as a security solution that can be applied universally, without addressing the fact that every MFA implementation today is Single-Factor Authentication (SFA) masquerading as MFA. Students are not taught to question how transmitted data, whether it's a password, token, or biometric data, can be intercepted, manipulated, or spoofed. Instead, they are told that simply adding more layers of transmitted data constitutes genuine MFA.

Genuine MFA requires distinct factors, such as something the user knows (password or PIN), something the user has (a physical digital ID), and something the user is (the state of being connected). Yet, this critical distinction is glossed over in favor of teaching students to implement vendor-driven solutions that rely solely on transmitted data. This misapplication of MFA in education leads professionals to *believe* that their systems are secure when, in fact, they remain vulnerable to all the exact same attacks that SFA systems face.

The Convenience-First Mindset

Another critical flaw in the cybersecurity education system is the emphasis on convenience over security. Many educational programs teach students to prioritize ease of implementation and user experience over the robustness of the security protocols being employed. While convenience is an important factor in user adoption, it should never come at the expense of security. Unfortunately, the convenience-first mindset has become so ingrained in the industry that it has led to compromised security protocols being accepted as standard practice.

This focus on convenience is particularly evident in the way that public access models are taught as acceptable security solutions. The decision to allow public access to secure networks was based on the need to provide easy access for users in the last century, but it also introduced a critical vulnerability that has never been addressed. Rather than teaching students to question the validity of public login MFA, the education system reinforces the idea that adding more layers of mitigation can compensate for the inherent weaknesses of public access models.

Producing Professionals Without Critical Thinking

The result is a generation of cybersecurity professionals who are more concerned with ensuring that their systems are easy to use, rather than teaching them how to truly secure a network. This mindset has led to a widespread acceptance of insecure solutions when the focus is placed on providing a good user experience. It has also stifled the innovation and critical thinking needed to develop new security models that prioritize binary security principles over convenience.

Refocusing on the Science of Security

To address the failures of the cybersecurity education system, a fundamental shift in how security is taught is needed. The first step is to refocus education on the science of security protocols, emphasizing the binary logic that governs all security decisions. Students must be taught that every decision in cybersecurity is either right or wrong and that there is no room for guessing when it comes to protecting sensitive systems.

Education programs must also prioritize critical thinking and problem-solving over product configuration. In addition to teaching students to implement specific tools, curricula should focus on helping students understand the underlying principles of network security, so they can evaluate the effectiveness of different solutions and propose their own innovations based on critical thinking.

Balancing Corporate Influence

Additionally, the influence of corporations on cybersecurity education must be balanced with the need to produce professionals who can think independently. While vendor tools are essential to network security, students must be taught to evaluate these tools critically and reject solutions that do not meet the binary standard of security. This will require a shift away from vendor-driven education and toward a more holistic approach that emphasizes the importance of binary security protocols over convenience.

Conclusion: Reforming Cybersecurity Education

The failures of the cybersecurity education system have contributed to the widespread insecurity that defines today's digital world. By focusing on product configuration and convenience over the science of security protocols, educational programs have produced professionals who are ill-equipped to meet the challenges of the modern threat landscape.

Reforming cybersecurity education is essential to producing professionals who can think critically, innovate, and demand real security solutions. By teaching students the binary logic that underpins all security decisions and by encouraging them to question flawed models, the industry can begin to rebuild the foundation of cybersecurity on principles of truth and integrity.

CHAPTER 7

The Rise of Mitigation: Patching Over the Problem

The foundation of the mitigation industry is the notion that security flaws can be patched rather than eliminated. This mindset emerged as public access models and transmitted-data-based MFA became the standard for network security, leaving systems vulnerable to breaches and exploits. Instead of rethinking the underlying models, the industry chose to mitigate these vulnerabilities by adding layers of security on top of existing flaws.

Treating Symptoms, Not Root Causes

The decision to embrace mitigation rather than addressing the root cause of insecurity has led to an ever-growing stack of security products designed to manage risk rather than eliminate the root cause. Organizations are sold firewalls, intrusion detection systems, encryption tools, and other products, all of which serve to mitigate the effects of potential breaches without addressing the core flaw: the reliance on public access and transmitted data.

© Christopher Murphy 2025
C. Murphy, *Digital Deception*, Apress Pocket Guides,
https://doi.org/10.1007/979-8-8688-1227-9_7

By choosing to treat symptoms rather than the root cause, the industry has created a system where security becomes increasingly complex and fragile. Each new mitigation solution adds another layer of complexity to the system, increasing the likelihood of misconfiguration and creating new opportunities for attackers. As systems become more complex, they become harder to secure, leading to an endless cycle of breaches, patches, and further breaches.

The False Sense of Security

The reliance on mitigation solutions has created a false sense of security for many organizations. By layering multiple security products on top of each other, organizations believe they are creating a robust defense against cyber threats. However, these layers are only patches; they do not address the fundamental vulnerability that exists in the system. As a result, organizations are lulled into a false sense of security, believing that their systems are protected when in fact they remain highly vulnerable.

This illusion of security is further reinforced by the marketing of mitigation products as comprehensive solutions. Vendors sell their products as essential components of a defense-in-depth strategy, promoting the idea that more layers equate to better security. In truth, the more layers that are added to a system, the more points of failure are introduced, and the more opportunities exist for cybercriminals to exploit the system's weaknesses.

Complexity As the Enemy of Security

The belief that complexity equals security has become deeply ingrained in the industry, leading organizations to continue piling on layers of mitigation without ever addressing the underlying vulnerability.

This approach has created a cybersecurity model where organizations are more focused on damage control than on preventing breaches in the first place.

The rise of the mitigation industry can be directly tied to the economic incentives that drive it. Vendors and cybersecurity firms have a vested interest in promoting mitigation solutions because they generate recurring revenue. Each new breach or vulnerability creates an opportunity to sell another layer of mitigation, creating a profitable cycle where the industry thrives on the very problems it claims to solve.

The Profitability of Mitigation

This business model is particularly lucrative because it allows vendors to sell multiple layers of security without ever providing a solution that truly eliminates risk. As long as the underlying vulnerability remains unaddressed, organizations will continue to buy mitigation products to manage their risk. This has led to an industry-wide focus on risk management rather than risk elimination, with many companies spending on cybersecurity products, but nothing addressing the root cause of their vulnerability.

The economic incentives behind mitigation also explain why the industry has been slow to adopt a private access model and genuine MFA. These solutions would eliminate many of the vulnerabilities that mitigation products are designed to address, reducing the need for complex security stacks and cutting into the profits of vendors that rely on selling multiple layers of mitigation. In other words, solving the core issues would eliminate much of the demand for products, which would negatively impact the bottom line of the industry.

The Consequences of Increasing Complexity

One of the most significant consequences of the mitigation-first mindset is the increasing complexity of cybersecurity systems. As organizations continue to add layers of mitigation to their networks, they create systems that are not only more difficult to secure but also more prone to misconfiguration and human error. The more layers that are added, the harder it becomes to manage, monitor, and secure the system as a whole.

This complexity creates new vulnerabilities, as each layer of mitigation introduces additional points of failure. Cybercriminals are adept at exploiting these weaknesses, often finding ways to bypass or compromise mitigation products. The more complex the system, the more opportunities there are for attackers to identify misconfigurations or loopholes that allow them to gain access to the network. When a hacker identifies a hole in one network, it opens the door for other corporate networks to be breached as well.

Delayed Detection and Increased Damage

In addition to increasing the risk of breaches, this complexity also makes it harder for organizations to detect when their systems have been compromised. With multiple layers of security products operating simultaneously, it can be difficult to identify where the breach occurred or how it was executed. This delayed detection allows attackers to remain in the system longer, causing more damage and stealing more data before the breach is identified and mitigated.

Ignoring Real Solutions

The rise of the mitigation industry has largely been fueled by the industry's refusal to adopt a private access model and genuine MFA. This solution would eliminate many of the vulnerabilities that mitigation products are designed to address, but they have been largely ignored in favor of more profitable strategies. The prevailing strategy remains patch the breach, pray it is sufficient, and repeat with each new exploit, guaranteeing continuing mitigation revenues.

The Simplicity of Private Access Models

A private access model, where only authorized users can interact with the system, would eliminate the need for public-facing logins, which are one of the primary points of entry for cybercriminals. By implementing digital IDs and existence-as-a-factor in genuine MFA, organizations could virtually eliminate the risk of unauthorized access and identity theft.

However, adopting this solution would require a fundamental shift in the way organizations approach security. Rather than relying on layered mitigation, organizations would need to embrace the binary logic of security protocols and design their systems with real security in mind from the outset. This shift would eliminate the need for many of the mitigation products currently being sold, and it would create a simpler, more secure system that is easier to manage and protect.

The End of Mitigation-First Strategies

The rise of mitigation solutions has created a cybersecurity industry where real security is sacrificed in favor of damage control. Rather than addressing the root cause of the vulnerability, the industry has focused on patching over problems, creating a system that is increasingly complex and fragile. This reliance on mitigation has created a false sense of security while allowing the economic incentives of the industry to take precedence over the need for real solutions.

Conclusion: A Path to Real Security

The time has come to move away from the mitigation-first mindset and embrace solutions that address the root cause of insecurity. A private access model and genuine MFA offer a pathway to simpler, more secure systems that do not require layers of mitigation to function effectively. By embracing this solution, organizations can break free from the cycle of breaches and patches and begin to build systems that are secure by design.

CHAPTER 8

The Failure to Look Beyond the Immediate Horizon

The cybersecurity crisis of today is not the result of a single failure but rather a series of shortsighted decisions driven by immediate convenience and profitability. Decision-makers, pressured by the need for quick fixes, often failed to consider the long-term consequences of their actions. This short-term thinking, a failure to look beyond the immediate horizon, has left the digital world vulnerable to escalating and more sophisticated threats. Instead of addressing the root cause of insecurity, the industry has chosen to patch over problems, allowing the mitigation industry to thrive by offering temporary solutions that perpetuate, rather than resolve, the crisis.

The Rise of Short-Term Thinking

The rise of short-term thinking in cybersecurity emerged as organizations quickly adopted Internet-based models during the early days of digital expansion. The focus was on providing seamless access to services and rapidly expanding the digital economy, while security was relegated to

© Christopher Murphy 2025
C. Murphy, *Digital Deception*, Apress Pocket Guides,
https://doi.org/10.1007/979-8-8688-1227-9_8

an afterthought. The prevailing mindset was that security concerns could be dealt with later, once convenience and user experience goals were achieved.

This approach quickly became entrenched as businesses, eager to stay ahead of the competition, embraced public access models and transmitted data for authentication. These models, while convenient, exposed networks to significant vulnerabilities. Instead of rethinking the underlying security architecture, the industry chose to pile on mitigation solutions, adding layer upon layer of complexity to patch over core weaknesses. This created a culture where quick fixes became the standard, and long-term security was left in the cold.

The Limitations of Mitigation

Mitigation, however, does nothing to address the root problem; it merely manages the damage until it can no longer be managed. Every new breach, hack, or exploit is treated with another layer of temporary fixes, creating a cycle where vulnerabilities are managed but never eliminated. This focus on damage control, rather than preventing breaches, reflects a systemic failure to address the root cause of insecurity: the reliance on public logins and transmitted data as the core of authentication.

Contrary to popular belief, real security solutions such as a private access model and genuine MFA are not inherently difficult to implement. These solutions are built on binary logic, which makes them elegantly simple and highly effective. The solution to the public access problem, private access, is not a technical challenge but rather a conceptual shift. Let me say that again so it really sinks in: private access is *not* a technical challenge but rather a conceptual shift. The perception that private access is disruptive, complex, or costly stems from misconceptions that have no basis in fact.

Understanding Private Access and Its Simplicity

Private access requires minimal changes to existing infrastructure because it affects the user interaction method, not the underlying network. Private access is completed before a secure network login is loaded. In other words, the solution is enacted when the network shifts its login model from public to private. This shift happens outside the network, making it fast, clean, effective, and, most importantly, secure.

The failure to understand this key distinction between public and private access affecting the interaction method rather than the infrastructure itself is where the misconceptions about difficulty, complexity, and disruption arise. Implementing private access and genuine MFA can be done without major overhauls to infrastructure, and it can operate concurrently. This makes the solution not only feasible but also regulatory compliant, with the science to prove both.

Misconceptions and Economic Incentives

The real barrier to adopting private access and genuine MFA is not technical complexity but the deeply ingrained misconceptions and preconceptions that have become entrenched in the cybersecurity mindset. These misconceptions perpetuate the false notion that current mitigation solutions are good enough and that more layers of security will eventually solve the problem.

In truth, every additional layer of mitigation increases the complexity and fragility of the system, introducing new points of failure. Instead of seeing the elegant simplicity of private access and digital IDs, many organizations are trapped by the belief that security must be complex to be effective. This is a fallacy. The binary nature of computer science makes it clear that a system is either secure or insecure; there is no middle ground. Adding more layers of complexity only makes the system harder to secure and more likely to fail.

The misconception that real security is difficult to implement has also been driven by the economic incentives of the mitigation industry. Remember, vendors and service providers profit from selling mitigation products, which thrive on the very vulnerabilities they fail to address. By promoting the idea that a private access model and genuine MFA are difficult, the industry perpetuates a cycle where mitigation is continually required, driving revenue while keeping systems inherently vulnerable.

The Cost of Short-Term Thinking

While mitigation solutions may provide temporary relief, the long-term costs of relying on short-term fixes have been devastating. The global economic impact of cybercrime is already estimated at $10 trillion annually, with that number projected to double in the next five years. Much of this damage can be traced back to the industry's reliance on flawed models and inadequate security solutions that treat symptoms rather than the root cause.

Breaking down $10 trillion in cyber damage into smaller time increments is an effective way to highlight the urgency for action. For example:

- **Per Year**: $10 trillion

- **Per Month**: $833 billion

- **Per Week**: $192 billion

- **Per Day**: $27.4 billion

- **Per Hour**: $1.14 billion

- **Per Minute**: $19 million

- **Per Second**: $316,000

This breakdown makes the staggering costs of cyber damage much more tangible and emphasizes the pressing need for immediate cybersecurity measures.

The Missed Opportunity for Real Security

Organizations that continue to invest in mitigation strategies rather than real security are setting themselves up for greater financial losses in the future. The longer the underlying vulnerability continues to remain unaddressed, the greater the risk of significant breaches that cause irreparable damage. Moreover, as the legal and regulatory landscape continues to evolve, companies that fail to adopt genuine MFA and a private access model may face growing liability and legal exposure.

The opportunity cost of ignoring real solutions is also staggering. Each day that organizations rely on public access and transmitted data, they are missing the opportunity to implement a private access model and existence-based MFA, both of which offer far more effective security without the need for endless layers of mitigation. The failure to adopt this solution means that organizations remain vulnerable, continuously patching over flaws that could be eliminated entirely with a simpler, more secure approach.

A Clear Path Forward

The path forward for the cybersecurity industry is clear: return to binary logic and embrace the simple solution that eliminates vulnerabilities at their core. A private access model and genuine MFA are not futuristic concepts; they are immediate solutions that can be deployed with minimal disruption at a fraction of the cost of maintaining complex mitigation stacks.

By embracing private access, organizations can close the door to unauthorized users entirely, eliminating the need for public-facing login pages that expose networks to identity guessing. Genuine MFA, which uses tangible digital IDs to introduce existence-as-a-factor, ensures that the person attempting to access the system is the authorized user, not just someone with the correct transmitted data.

Conclusion: Eliminating the Short-Term Mindset

The failure to look beyond the immediate horizon has left the cybersecurity industry mired in a cycle of short-term fixes and mitigation. However, the belief that real security solutions are difficult to deploy is a gross misconception. The true barrier is not complexity but preconceptions that have no basis in fact.

Private access and genuine MFA offer a clear, simple solution to the cybersecurity crisis, one that eliminates vulnerabilities at their root rather than merely treating the symptoms. By embracing the binary logic of security, the industry can move beyond its reliance on mitigation, adopting solutions that provide real, lasting protection. The time to abandon short-term thinking is now.

CHAPTER 9

The Internet As a Crime Scene

The Internet, once envisioned as a platform for global communication and information sharing, has morphed into a crime scene, not because of a singular failure but because of thousands of small compromises made over decades. Many of these decisions were made with the best of intentions, while others were driven by short-term profit and convenience. Regardless of the motives, the result is an Internet plagued by deception, insecurity, and constant threats.

From Closed Networks to Public Access

In its early days, the Internet evolved from private, closed networks designed for secure data exchange. Throughout the 1970s and 1980s, these systems were simple but secure, closed to unauthorized access and limited to authorized personnel working in controlled environments. There was no need for public access. Everything was local, and the infrastructure was inherently secure.

This all changed when businesses joined the WWW, transforming it from a network for research into a public platform. This shift marked a critical moment, a bifurcation that set the stage for today's cybersecurity crisis. Public access became the default mode of interaction, and with it came the need for public logins to access sensitive information and

© Christopher Murphy 2025
C. Murphy, *Digital Deception*, Apress Pocket Guides,
https://doi.org/10.1007/979-8-8688-1227-9_9

perform secure activities. This was the first major compromise, the moment when secure systems were opened to the public, fundamentally weakening their defenses.

The Introduction of Public Logins

By introducing public logins for what should have remained private systems, the perfect conditions for cybercrime were established, over three decades ago. What was once closed and secure was now wide open and vulnerable. The assumption that a public login screen could secure access to a private network represented a fundamental misunderstanding of how security protocols should be applied.

In the early 1990s, as the Internet began to expand, decisions were made based on the technology of the time and a desire to make the Web more accessible to a growing number of users. Security was treated as a necessary evil, something that could be dealt with later, once the technology caught up to the scale of the Web.

Convenience over Security

As personal computers became more prevalent in businesses, security protocols took on greater importance, but they were still seen as a secondary consideration. Early security models were designed with accessibility and availability (convenience) in mind, not security. This guiding principle would dominate the cybersecurity industry until today, prioritizing user experience over genuine protection.

Decisions to prioritize public access led to a cascade of security compromises. From the introduction of login systems for sensitive activities to the proliferation of password-based security models, each step represented a move away from the binary truth: either a system is secure (private), or it is not (public).

Guessing Identity: The Core Flaw

At the heart of the Internet's transformation into a crime scene was the decision to grant public access to secure networks. This model allowed anonymous entities on the Web to submit data to what were once private data silos, forcing systems to rely on guesses about user identity.

This decision created a fundamental flaw in how security was handled. Instead of focusing on proving identity, systems were designed to guess identity based on transmitted data. The failure to adopt a private access model, where digital IDs directly confirm the user's identity, has led to today's endless cycle of breaches, mitigation patches, and escalating cybercrime.

Profit over Protection

As businesses prioritized profit potential over security, early leaders in the industry failed to address the growing vulnerabilities created by public login access. Security was seen as a cost center rather than an opportunity for innovation. This mindset prevented the industry from taking action to correct the flaw in the system.

Rather than acknowledging the vulnerability, the industry chose to ignore the problem, believing that patching solutions and mitigation layers would suffice. This short-term thinking created the perfect environment for cybercriminals to exploit. Every breach became another opportunity to add layers of mitigation, further entrenching the flawed model rather than addressing the root cause.

The Growing Threat of Cybercrime

As breaches grew more common, the decision to mitigate rather than solve became the industry's guiding principle. The cybersecurity sector grew around the idea that convenience should be prioritized over the binary truth of security: that secure activity must never be public.

As the Web continued to evolve, so did the opportunities for cybercriminals. What began as small-scale breaches soon grew into a global industry of cybercrime, with hackers targeting everything from financial institutions to governments.

The same vulnerability created by public login access remained unaddressed, and cybercriminals were quick to take advantage. Today, cybercrime exceeds $10 trillion in damages, with projections showing that this figure will only rise as more people and organizations fall victim to the flawed systems that remain in place.

The Compounding Problem of Mitigation

The failure to address the root cause (public login access) has led to an explosion of security failures. Each patch introduced to solve one problem creates new opportunities for misconfiguration and exploitation, compounding the issue further with every step.

The path to the Internet becoming a crime scene stems from the decision to grant public access to what should have been private networks from the very beginning. From that moment on, the Internet's security model was fundamentally broken. Every compromise, every patch, and every mitigation layer has pushed the industry further from the binary truth of security.

The Binary Truth of Security

At its core, security is always binary. Either a system is secure, or it is not. And every decision to patch, rather than correct the original error of public access, has only deepened the crisis. The solution is not more layers of complexity or more mitigation strategies. The solution is a return to a private access model, where digital IDs and direct user interaction provide the binary security needed to protect systems and networks.

The Oversight of Internet Architects

One of the Internet's founding fathers, Vint Cerf, acknowledged the security oversights in the Internet's design, admitting that security was an afterthought. Cerf said, "Looking back on it, I don't know whether it would have worked out to try to incorporate... this key-distribution system," adding, "We might not have been able to get much traction to adopt and use the network, because it would have been too difficult." This statement underscores the challenge faced by early Internet architects: balancing usability with security. However, the persistence of this oversight, decades later, illustrates a more profound issue within the cybersecurity community. Even as the flaws became evident, the industry continued to rely on bolted-on security measures rather than rethinking the fundamental design while it was still in its infancy.

Breaking the Cycle

This acknowledgment by Cerf serves as a poignant example of how blind conformity can perpetuate a fundamental flaw. Even those who shaped the Internet have found themselves adhering to outdated models, reinforcing a system that prioritizes convenience over true security. The challenge now is to break free from this cycle, to recognize that the Internet's current state as a crime scene is not an immutable fate but a consequence of choices made and, thus, choices that can be unmade.

A Return to Binary Principles

As we move forward, the path to correcting this error lies in embracing the original vision of secure, private networks. The Internet was not doomed to become a crime scene; it was allowed to become one through a series of avoidable decisions. By returning to binary principles and implementing private access, we can reclaim the Internet's potential as a safe, trusted platform for global communication and commerce. Unfortunately, the years of damage and exploitation cannot be undone, but they can be halted if we act and change the path.

CHAPTER 10

Regulatory Failures and the Consequences of Inaction

The Role of Regulators in Cybersecurity

While the cybersecurity industry has evolved, the role of regulators enforcing compliance and ensuring the deployment of real security solutions has been virtually nonexistent. Despite clear standards, such as the FFIEC's 2006 "By definition true MFA," regulators have turned a blind eye to widespread noncompliance, choosing not to enforce the binary standards required for real security. This failure to act has not only allowed companies to falsify compliance but has also contributed directly to the cybersecurity crisis we face today.

© Christopher Murphy 2025
C. Murphy, *Digital Deception*, Apress Pocket Guides,
https://doi.org/10.1007/979-8-8688-1227-9_10

The FFIEC's 2006 MFA Standard

The FFIEC's 2006 definition of true MFA was a clear attempt to set the standard for secure authentication. It recognized that transmitted-data-based authentication, like Single-Factor Authentication (SFA), was inadequate for securing sensitive information and protecting users. The standard required more than one distinct factor to qualify as MFA. Yet, despite this, regulators have failed to enforce these binary standards in any meaningful way.

A First-Hand Example of Regulatory Failure

In 2020, the author of this book directly presented a genuine MFA solution to the FFIEC, seeking recognition that the solution met the very standards they had laid out years prior. Instead of confirming this compliance, the FFIEC refused to take a position on the technology, stating that their agency "does not take sides" on specific technologies. This refusal to acknowledge compliance, despite it being aligned with their own regulation, demonstrates a profound failure of regulatory bodies to do their job.

The consequences of this regulatory inaction are clear: companies have continued to claim MFA compliance without meeting the standards set forth by the FFIEC in 2006, and the cybersecurity industry has become dominated by false solutions. The regulators, who should have been enforcing real security, have instead allowed the industry to perpetuate deceptive claims, contributing to the staggering levels of cyber damage we see today.

The Spread of Public Access Models

The failure of regulators like the FFIEC to enforce genuine MFA has allowed public access models to become the norm for network security. These models, by their very nature, introduce vulnerabilities that no amount of mitigation can truly address. Yet, rather than correcting the problem, regulators have consistently allowed organizations to use SFA masquerading as MFA, relying on mitigation strategies to patch over the flaws.

This inaction has resulted in a cybersecurity environment where breaches are not only expected but accepted as inevitable. The reliance on public access and transmitted data for authentication has made networks inherently insecure, but regulators have been content to let companies continue with false claims of security. Every breach, every ransomware attack, and every data leak could have been prevented *if* regulators had enforced the binary standards set forth in their own guidelines published in 2006.

A Missed Opportunity to Enforce Real Security

The author's direct experience with the FFIEC highlights the regulatory failure at the heart of this crisis. When the FFIEC refused to confirm compliance because they chose "not to take a side," they were effectively stating that they did not want to confirm any technology compliant because... they would have to acknowledge that not one deployment of MFA, even their own, was in fact... (wait for it) *compliant* with their own standards as set forth. This was another critical moment and a missed opportunity to enforce real security to address the ever-growing crisis. The refusal to acknowledge a solution existed not only undermined the regulation itself but also demonstrated how regulatory bodies have actively facilitated and participated in the deception we experience today.

Consequences Beyond the Financial Sector

The consequences of regulatory failure are not confined to the financial sector. The author's interactions with other regulatory bodies, including those governing healthcare, government, and critical infrastructure, reveal a similar pattern of inaction. Regulators have consistently chosen not to enforce the standards that would have protected users and secured networks, instead allowing mitigation-based solutions to dominate.

This domino effect has resulted in a cybersecurity industry that is built on false claims, with organizations across all sectors believing they are secure when, in fact, they are not. The failure of regulators to enforce real security has created a global vulnerability that continues to grow with each passing year.

The Disconnect Between Standards and Enforcement

One of the key failures of the regulatory environment has been the disconnect between setting standards and enforcing them. Regulators like the FFIEC may issue guidelines and regulations that define what genuine MFA looks like, but without enforcement, these guidelines become aspirational rather than mandatory. This disconnect has allowed companies to claim compliance with MFA standards while using the exact same model they used before "By definition true MFA" was written.

The failure to bridge the gap between standards and enforcement has enabled the entire industry to engage in a form of self-deception, convincing itself and its customers that the security being provided is adequate, when in fact it is woefully insufficient. The regulators, by failing to act, have contributed directly to this deception.

The Economic and Social Costs of Inaction

To move beyond the current cybersecurity crisis, regulators must take an active role in enforcing real security solutions. The days of allowing public access models and false MFA claims must come to an end. Regulatory bodies like the FFIEC need to acknowledge the binary nature of security and enforce the standards they set almost two decades ago.

Enforcing a private access model and genuine MFA is not just a matter of regulation but a matter of global security. The economic and social costs of continued inaction are too great to ignore. The time for regulatory bodies to stand by and refuse to take sides has passed; the world needs them to act.

The Impact of Regulatory Failures

The failure of regulators to enforce real security is not just an oversight; it is a choice. By refusing to enforce binary standards, regulators have allowed the cybersecurity crisis to grow into a global problem, with economic and legal consequences that will continue to mount. The author's experience with the FFIEC is just one example of how regulatory inaction has contributed to the problem.

The inaction by regulatory bodies has broader implications than just compliance failure. This lack of enforcement has allowed the cybersecurity landscape to be shaped by those who profit from its vulnerabilities. An article by Business Insider quoting Vint Cerf, one of the "fathers of the Internet," highlighted that the Internet was born with two big flaws, and lots of little ones, like the lack of security and the lack of authentication mechanisms built into its foundation. Cerf admitted that "security was an afterthought" and that early efforts to incorporate a more secure architecture might not have gained traction because of the perceived complexity.

Correcting the Foundation

Cerf's reflections underscore the missed opportunities by regulatory bodies to enforce a secure foundation. Instead of addressing these inherent flaws as the Internet grew, regulators allowed the market to dictate security practices. This resulted in the layering of security measures over an insecure foundation, rather than correcting the foundational issue itself. The result is a system that is inherently insecure, propped up by patchwork solutions that fail to address the root cause.

The recognition of these flaws by one of the Internet's creators should have prompted regulatory bodies to act more decisively. Yet, the continued reliance on mitigation strategies and the reluctance to enforce genuine security measures have perpetuated the problem. Regulators have a responsibility to enforce standards that address these foundational flaws, yet they have consistently chosen to allow the industry to operate without real oversight.

Conclusion: The Path Forward

As the cybersecurity crisis deepens, the role of regulators must shift from passive observers to active enforcers. The industry can no longer afford to operate on the assumption that public access models and mitigation strategies are sufficient. By enforcing the adoption of a private access model and digital IDs, regulators can begin to correct the course and restore security to the Internet.

The path to rebuilding trust and security starts with acknowledging the regulatory failures that have allowed this crisis to unfold. The time for inaction is over. Regulators must enforce the standards they have set and hold organizations accountable for implementing real security solutions. Only by doing so can we hope to end the cycle of breaches and build a more secure digital world.

CHAPTER 11

The Role of Vendors and Auditors in Perpetuating the Cybersecurity Crisis

The cybersecurity crisis has not been driven solely by the failures of regulators or the blind conformity of organizations. A significant contributor to the ongoing problem is the role played by cybersecurity vendors and auditors. These entities, whether through intentional actions or negligence, have helped perpetuate the deception surrounding Multi-Factor Authentication (MFA) compliance and have profited from selling solutions that fall far short of meeting genuine MFA standards. Their actions have created a system where the illusion of security masks widespread vulnerabilities.

Vendors and False MFA Solutions

Cybersecurity vendors have played a critical role in the spread of false MFA claims by marketing products that claim to be secure but fail to meet the binary standards of genuine MFA. These vendors, eager to meet the

© Christopher Murphy 2025
C. Murphy, *Digital Deception*, Apress Pocket Guides,
https://doi.org/10.1007/979-8-8688-1227-9_11

growing demand for convenient security solutions, have often chosen
to sell products based on transmitted data, ignoring the fundamental
requirement for more than one distinct factor in authentication. This
decision to market Single-Factor Authentication (SFA) products as MFA is
more than just a marketing strategy; it is a form of deception.

Many vendors are fully aware that their products do not meet the
requirements for genuine MFA. Some vendors have even gone so far as to
correct their marketing claims to stipulate multi-*step* authentication, all
the while continuing to sell the same deceptive products to organizations
across all sectors, falsely claiming compliance with regulatory standards.
By doing so, they contribute directly to the chain of deception that exposes
both companies and users to massive security vulnerabilities. This focus
on convenience reflects a broader trend within the industry: prioritizing
profit over real security.

Mitigation Products over Real Solutions

Rather than investing in true solutions that require more significant shifts
in user interaction models, vendors have relied on mitigation products that
mask the underlying security flaw. This approach not only keeps vendor
profits flowing but also ensures that their clients remain trapped in a cycle
of dependency on continuous patches and upgrades, rather than solving
the core problem. As long as the vendors can continue selling quick
fixes, the real vulnerabilities in network security remain unaddressed,
perpetuating the very crisis they claim to combat.

Auditors: Legitimizing False Security

While vendors engaged in selling deceptive solutions, auditors have played
a crucial role in giving these solutions an air of legitimacy. Auditors, whose
responsibility is to ensure that companies are complying with regulatory

standards, have failed to uphold their duty. Instead, they have certified systems as compliant even though these systems do not meet genuine MFA requirements. The result is that many organizations believe they are secure when, in fact, they are far from it.

The KPMG Evaluation: A Case Study

The 2020 evaluation by KPMG exemplifies how auditors have played a direct role in perpetuating this deception. KPMG provided a steeply discounted valuation for the author's patented private access solution, which introduced a genuine MFA system based on private access and digital IDs. The justification KPMG offered was that "compliance would not drive adoption," essentially assuring companies that they had little incentive to adopt real security solutions even if they were made aware of their noncompliance.

What is more troubling, however, is KPMG's failure to inform their clients of this critical compliance issue. This omission left sectors such as healthcare and finance particularly vulnerable, as organizations in these industries rely heavily on robust authentication systems to protect sensitive data. Without awareness of the compliance gaps, these clients continued to operate with a false sense of security, exposing themselves to significant risks and breaches. With full knowledge of the binary nature of genuine MFA and the inadequacy of the current systems in place, KPMG either deliberately withheld this information or misrepresented the compliance status to their clients. Whether this failure was through omission or active misrepresentation, KPMG ensured that their clients remained unaware or unmotivated to address the serious compliance issues within their security infrastructure.

Economic Incentives Driving Complicity

At the heart of vendor and auditor complicity in this crisis are the
economic incentives that drive their actions. Vendors profit from selling
mitigation solutions that offer short-term fixes to long-term problems,
while auditors benefit from maintaining ongoing relationships with clients
who rely on their certifications to demonstrate compliance. The financial
interests of these entities take precedence over addressing the actual
security flaws that leave companies and users vulnerable.

By promoting false solutions, both vendors and auditors have created
an ecosystem where security is treated as a product to be sold, rather
than an absolute standard to be met. This focus on profitability has led
to the widespread adoption of inadequate security measures. Instead of
implementing real security solutions, companies are forced to pay more
for patches and upgrades that do nothing to address the root cause of the
problem.

The Cycle of Dependency

The mitigation industry thrives on the complexity of the current cybersecurity
landscape. Every breach, every hack, and every new vulnerability creates an
opportunity for vendors to sell more products and for auditors to perform
more reviews, all while the core issue of public access remains unresolved.
This cycle of dependency ensures that vendors and auditors continue to profit
from the crisis, while businesses and users pay the price.

The Growing List of Victims

As discussed in previous chapters, the chain of deception is long and
continues to grow with every false claim of compliance. Vendors and
auditors are at the center of this chain, creating and perpetuating a false

sense of security that exposes organizations and Internet users to real risk. For every company that buys into these false solutions, there are countless users whose data is left vulnerable, creating a cascading effect of harm.

The victims of this deception are not just the companies themselves but also the customers, employees, patients, and users who trust these systems to protect their sensitive information. Each failure in security results in more personal data exposed, more identity theft, and more financial losses, all of which could have been prevented by the adoption of a genuine MFA solution.

Breaking the Cycle of Deception

To break this cycle of deception and complicity, business leaders must begin holding both vendors and auditors accountable for their role in perpetuating the crisis. Vendors must be required to sell genuinely compliant solutions, like private access and true MFA, rather than relying on transmitted-data-based systems that offer no real security. Similarly, auditors must be held to higher standards, ensuring that the systems they certify meet the binary requirements for true security.

This accountability must extend beyond simple regulatory fines or settlements. The entire cybersecurity ecosystem must undergo a transformation where real security solutions become the standard and the vendors and auditors who perpetuate false claims are no longer allowed to dominate the market. Without this change, the chain of victims will continue to grow, and the cybersecurity crisis will only worsen.

Conclusion: Holding Vendors and Auditors Accountable

The role of vendors and auditors in perpetuating the cybersecurity crisis is clear. By focusing on profit-driven security, they have chosen to ignore the binary nature of real security and have instead profited from selling and certifying false and inadequate solutions. This behavior has created a chain of deception that leaves both companies and Internet users vulnerable to massive risk.

To move forward, the industry must demand more from those responsible for securing our networks. Vendors must stop selling convenience and start providing real security, and auditors must stop certifying systems that do not meet the standards for genuine MFA as set forth by the FFIEC and NIST. Only by addressing the root cause of the problem can we hope to break the cycle and create a cybersecurity landscape that truly protects those it is meant to serve.

CHAPTER 12

The Victims of Cybersecurity Deception: Internet Users and the Global Economy

The Burden on Everyday Users

At the heart of the cybersecurity crisis are the real victims: everyday Internet users and the global economy. While corporations, auditors, and vendors have profited from false security claims and ineffective mitigation solutions, the cost of this deception has been passed onto consumers through higher prices, increased fees, and uncontrolled data breaches. Despite the billions spent on mitigation strategies, firewalls, and authentication products, the burden of these failures falls squarely on the shoulders of those the system is supposed to protect: the users.

© Christopher Murphy 2025
C. Murphy, *Digital Deception*, Apress Pocket Guides,
https://doi.org/10.1007/979-8-8688-1227-9_12

The Staggering Cost of Cybercrime

The magnitude of cybercrime damage is now staggering. It exceeds $10 trillion annually, with projections suggesting it could double within the next five years. This financial burden is not shouldered by the corporations responsible for cybersecurity shortcomings; instead, it is passed on to consumers through higher prices and hidden fees. Internet users find themselves footing the bill for a system that consistently fails to protect them, exacerbating the very vulnerabilities it claims to secure.

False Promises of Security

Every individual who uses the Internet, whether for banking, shopping, or communication, has become a victim of a system built on false security promises. The reliance on public access models, transmitted data, and deceptive Multi-Factor Authentication (MFA) claims has left billions of users exposed to data breaches, identity theft, and the relentless risk of having their personal information exploited by malicious actors. These users unknowingly pay the price for a broken system that pretends to safeguard them yet fails to provide real security.

The Overlooked Victims

For too long, cybersecurity efforts have focused on protecting organizations' networks and infrastructure, overlooking the true victims: the individual users whose personal data is at risk with every breach. This failure stems from the industry's decision to open public access to secure networks, a choice that has exposed every Internet user to potential identity guessing, data theft, and exploitation. Whether it's a retail breach, a healthcare hack, or a banking theft, each time personal information is compromised, the true cost of that decision becomes painfully clear.

The Illusion of MFA

What's worse is that Internet users have been made to believe they are protected. They are told that the systems they interact with are secure, thanks to the supposed implementation of MFA. Yet, these MFA systems are often nothing more than Single-Factor Authentication (SFA) masquerading as something more. The result? Users, through no fault of their own, are left vulnerable, convinced they are safe while being exposed to the growing risk of data breaches.

The Financial Fallout

The financial consequences of this cybersecurity crisis are staggering. With cybercrime damage exceeding $300,000 per second, the global economy has been deeply affected by the failure to implement a real security solution. Organizations continue to choose mitigation strategies over addressing the root cause of insecurity, and they offload the costs of their failures onto their customers in several ways:

- **Higher Prices**: Companies raise the cost of goods and services to compensate for the financial damage of cybercrime.

- **Increased Fees**: Banks and other financial institutions impose fees on users, masking them as necessary administrative costs when they are a direct consequence of cyber breaches.

- **Eroding Trust**: As more users experience breaches, trust in the digital economy erodes, leading to reduced participation in online services and slower economic growth.

The Cost per User

The average cost of cybercrime per user is staggering. With an estimated five billion Internet users worldwide, the damage translates to around $2,000 per person annually. This financial burden isn't paid by the corporations responsible for cybersecurity failures but is passed directly onto the victims they have created. They are the ones who absorb the costs of data breaches, identity theft, and deception, often while unknowingly purchasing security products from the same companies responsible for the vulnerabilities in the first place.

The Vicious Cycle of Exploitation

The irony of today's cybersecurity landscape is that users are often paying for security products that fail to protect them and, in fact, are part of the problem. Companies that market MFA solutions are selling false promises of security, pushing users to buy into deceptive systems that do nothing to protect their data. This creates a vicious cycle of exploitation: users are repeatedly victimized, first by criminals who steal their data, then by vendors who sell them ineffective solutions.

A Business Model Built on Deception

These deceivers, by selling false solutions, knowingly or unknowingly, create vulnerabilities that lead to data breaches, only to turn around and sell more products to protect users from the very threats they introduced. The cybersecurity industry has created a business model based on deception, selling users security products that don't address the core vulnerability in the system, leaving them even more exposed as before.

Economic Consequences for the Global Economy

The broader consequences of cybersecurity deception extend beyond the direct victims of breaches. The global economy bears the brunt of this damage. As cybercrime costs rise, the financial burden spreads across industries, leading to inflation, higher operational costs, reduced consumer spending, and slower economic growth. The digital economy, once a symbol of innovation and progress, is now plagued by the erosion of trust caused by false security claims and continuous breaches.

The Erosion of Trust in the Digital Economy

One of the most damaging aspects of cybersecurity deception is the loss of trust in the digital economy. As users become more aware of the vulnerabilities in the systems they use, they lose faith in the promises made by organizations. This loss of trust has long-term implications for the growth of the digital economy. Users, hesitant to engage in online transactions or share personal information, contribute to a chilling effect on innovation and growth.

The digital economy thrives on users' willingness to share their data and engage in commerce online. When that trust is broken, it creates a chilling effect on both innovation and economic activity. As more users experience the fallout of cybercrime, they may choose to reduce their online footprint, leading to decreased participation in online services and a slowdown in the adoption of new technologies.

Real Security Solutions

To break this cycle of victimization, the industry must shift away from
deceptive security models and implement real solutions. The adoption of a
private access model and genuine MFA is the only way to protect Internet
users from the growing threat of cybercrime. These solutions eliminate the
vulnerabilities introduced by public access models and provide the binary
security necessary to restore trust in the digital economy.

A Call to Action

Organizations must recognize that their responsibility extends beyond
protecting their own networks; they must ensure their users are genuinely
protected. This requires a commitment to true security, not just the
appearance of compliance. By adopting private access and genuine
MFA, companies can close the door to unauthorized users and offer the
protection that Internet users deserve.

Conclusion: Safeguarding the Victims

Until real security solutions are implemented, the chain of victims will only
continue to grow. Every breach, every instance of identity theft, and every
data leak serve as stark reminders of a system that is fundamentally flawed.
The true cost of these failures is borne by Internet users and the global
economy alike.

To truly protect users and restore trust in the digital economy, the
industry must embrace genuine security solutions. Only then can we put
an end to the endless cycle of breaches and exploitation, safeguarding the
real victims of the cybersecurity crisis and creating a digital world that can
be trusted once again.

CHAPTER 13

The Long Road to Correction: An Elegantly Simple Solution

Introduction: Addressing the Root Problem

The journey to resolve the cybersecurity crisis begins with an elegantly simple solution, one that requires no disruption to the network infrastructure. The core of the problem has never been the network itself but a fundamental issue with user interaction. The introduction of digital IDs and direct user interaction corrects the root problem without the need for a complete overhaul of network security. This realization places the cybersecurity industry at a pivotal moment: address the source of the error, and begin to untangle the unnecessary layers of mitigation that have complicated cybersecurity for decades.

© Christopher Murphy 2025
C. Murphy, *Digital Deception*, Apress Pocket Guides,
https://doi.org/10.1007/979-8-8688-1227-9_13

The Simplicity of the Solution

The solution is surprisingly straightforward. It has nothing to do with the network infrastructure, which is where many organizations focus their security efforts. Instead, the problem lies entirely in how user authentication is handled. The use of public access models for secure network logins has created an environment where guessing identity is the norm.

By implementing digital IDs issued to authorized users and requiring direct interaction between the user and the system, public logins can be eliminated altogether. This ensures that only users with the proper digital ID can access the network, removing the reliance on transmitted data and public access models.

Transitioning to Private Access

The beauty of this solution is that it doesn't require changes to the network's infrastructure. The network remains intact, and the login process simply shifts from a public model to a private one. This transition not only simplifies the system but makes it inherently more secure by adhering to binary security principles: either a user is authorized, or they are not. This eliminates guessing identity or relying on data transmission alone.

The Problem with Mitigation Solutions

The complexity of today's cybersecurity environment is largely due to the mitigation solutions layered on top of the flawed public access model. These products were designed to patch vulnerabilities created by public logins, but they are inherently flawed because they manage problems rather than fixing them.

Once digital IDs and a private access model are introduced, many of these mitigation solutions become unnecessary. The root problem, public logins to secure networks, is solved, rendering many of these products irrelevant. The industry has become so focused on managing public access risks that it has created an entire ecosystem of solutions that fail to address the root cause.

Simplifying the Security Stack

As organizations begin to adopt digital IDs and direct interaction, the next step on the road to correction is to untangle the web of mitigation solutions. Each layer of mitigation, whether it's firewalls, two-factor authentication, or monitoring software, was added to compensate for the public access flaw. Once private access is in place, these layers become redundant, and the security stack can be simplified, making systems not only more secure but easier to manage.

Cost Efficiency of the Solution

One of the most surprising aspects of this solution is that it's substantially less expensive than maintaining the layers of unnecessary mitigation products currently in use. Organizations have been spending billions of dollars on cybersecurity solutions designed to manage flaws introduced by public logins and identity guessing. Addressing the root cause drastically reduces these security costs.

Deploying digital IDs and a private access model is far less expensive than continuously purchasing and maintaining mitigation products designed to perpetuate sales of more mitigation products. Every additional layer of security mitigation adds to the operational cost of maintaining a network, firewalls, endpoint security, and monitoring systems that all contribute to an ever-increasing budget without solving the issue of public access.

Resolving User Authentication Challenges

At the heart of the cybersecurity crisis lies a user authentication problem, not a network infrastructure problem. The widespread use of public access models for secure network access has forced networks to rely on transmitted data to verify identity, turning the authentication process into a guessing game.

Shifting to a private access model that requires digital IDs makes user authentication a binary decision: either the user has the digital ID and is authorized, or they do not. This eliminates the need for identity guessing and ensures that only authorized users can access the network.

Enhancing MFA with a Third Factor

However, it is crucial to recognize that while digital IDs satisfy two factors of MFA (something the user has and something the user is, as the ID must be physically connected), they are not enough to guarantee complete security. Without the third factor, something the user knows, such as a password, PIN, or any other transmitted data, the system remains vulnerable if the ID is lost or stolen.

While digital IDs meet the legal standard for MFA and eliminate the legal exposure from current SFA systems masquerading as MFA, true security requires the third factor. Without this "knows" factor, anyone in possession of a stolen or lost ID could potentially access the system.

In the correct MFA model, users must still provide something they know, such as a password or PIN, in addition to possessing the digital ID and physically connecting it to the system. This ensures that even if the ID is lost, unauthorized users cannot access the system without the third factor.

Dismantling the Security Stack

Once a private access model is in place, the long road to correction becomes a process of dismantling the complex security stack built around public access. Each layer of security, added to mitigate vulnerabilities created by public logins, can be systematically removed.

Firewalls, two-factor authentication, endpoint security, and monitoring tools were all designed to manage the risks of public access. Once private access is implemented, many of these solutions become redundant. The network no longer needs to compensate for flaws introduced by public logins, as user authentication becomes binary and secure.

Benefits of Simplification

Dismantling the security stack will not only reduce costs but improve efficiency. Fewer layers of mitigation reduce opportunities for misconfiguration and exploits. By simplifying the security model, organizations can improve their overall security posture while reducing their reliance on expensive and unnecessary solutions.

A Path Toward Binary Security

The long road to correction does not involve adding more complexity; it requires simplification. By addressing the user authentication problem through digital IDs and a private access model, the cybersecurity industry can finally move away from the public login model that has caused so much damage.

The path forward involves reducing the number of mitigation products, simplifying the security stack, and focusing on binary security principles. The solution is not to continue piling on more layers of complexity but to strip away unnecessary tools and focus on correctly authenticating users.

Conclusion: Embracing an Elegantly Simple Solution

The long road to correction begins with an elegantly simple solution: digital IDs and a private access model. This approach addresses the root cause of the cybersecurity crisis without disrupting network infrastructure. Once digital IDs are in place, most mitigation products become unnecessary, simplifying the security stack and making networks inherently more secure.

The time for mitigation is over. The solution is clear: fix the user authentication problem with digital IDs, and the need for layers of security to manage public access vulnerabilities disappear. The path forward is one of simplicity and security, and it's time the industry embraced it.

CHAPTER 14

Corporate Leadership's Role in Cybersecurity: The Cost of Complacency and the Call for Accountability

Introduction: A Leadership Challenge

For far too long, corporate leadership has viewed cybersecurity as a problem that could be outsourced or delegated, rather than as a core responsibility to be owned and understood at the executive level. This complacency has fostered a culture of mitigation and false compliance, where executives have placed their trust in vendors and cybersecurity teams without fully comprehending the deeper issues. The result has been

© Christopher Murphy 2025
C. Murphy, *Digital Deception*, Apress Pocket Guides,
https://doi.org/10.1007/979-8-8688-1227-9_14

a systemic failure across industries, where organizations focus on patching problems rather than solving them, leaving themselves vulnerable to breaches and regulatory sanctions.

Early Complacency and Its Consequences

This complacency initially made sense during the early days of the Internet, when cyber threats were not fully understood and rapid business growth was the priority. The Internet was seen as a tool for innovation and expansion, not as a potential gateway for cyber threats. Security was an afterthought, and the prevailing belief was that any issues could be managed as they arose. This mindset allowed organizations to scale quickly, but it also laid the groundwork for the systemic vulnerabilities we see today.

The Illusion of Security Through Vendors

As the complexity and severity of cyberattacks have evolved, so too should corporate leadership's approach to cybersecurity. Relying on third-party vendors to manage security without oversight has created a false sense of security. Corporate leaders have wrongly assumed that paying for cybersecurity services equates to protection itself, believing that their investment in mitigation strategies, such as firewalls, two-factor authentication, and monitoring tools, was sufficient to safeguard their networks.

The MFA Deception and Its Impact

The reality is much harsher. The vendors corporate leaders trust has perpetuated the MFA deception, advocating for mitigation-first approaches that add layers of complexity without ever addressing the root problem. Public access models and Single-Factor Authentication (SFA) masquerading as Multi-Factor Authentication (MFA) continue to be at the core of these vulnerabilities. So long as public login is the foundation of network security, no amount of mitigation can provide true protection. Corporate leaders who rely on this illusion of security are setting their organizations up for failure.

The Cost of Complacency

The cost of this complacency is immense. Organizations that continue to operate under the false pretense of SFA-based MFA expose themselves to an increasing risk of breaches and legal liabilities. As the public becomes more aware of the MFA deception, companies that fail to implement real security solutions will face heightened scrutiny from regulators, lawsuits from affected customers, and a tarnished reputation. The financial cost of addressing this flaw now is far lower than the damage and liabilities that result from continued inaction.

Cybersecurity As a Leadership Responsibility

Cybersecurity is not just an IT issue; it is a leadership issue. Executives and board members must take ownership of understanding the fundamental principles of cybersecurity, ensuring their organizations adopt real security measures. This begins with acknowledging that the current system, built on public access models and false MFA compliance, is fundamentally broken.

The Failure of Delegation

The traditional approach of delegating cybersecurity to IT departments
or vendors has proven to be dangerously inadequate. Corporate leaders
have, in many cases, lost control over critical decisions that impact their
organization's security posture. This detachment has fostered a culture of
complacency, allowing security decisions to be made without the active
involvement of those who should understand the full scope of the risks
involved.

Embracing Binary Security Principles

To make meaningful changes, corporate leadership must embrace the
binary nature of security. Either a system is secure, or it is not. This binary
understanding underscores the illusion that mitigation solutions, which
simply add layers of temporary fixes, are not sufficient to secure a network.
The fundamental issue, public access to secure networks, remains
unresolved. So long as a public login remains in place, no system is truly
protected.

Implementing Genuine Security Measures

The solution is clear: a private access model and digital IDs that provide
genuine MFA. Corporate leaders must demand that their organizations
implement these solutions, ensuring that only authorized users can
interact with their system. This means moving away from the false comfort
of patching vulnerabilities and instead, addressing the core issue head-on
by eliminating public access and guesswork in identity verification.

Active Engagement in Security Decisions

Corporate leaders must also take an active role in evaluating the
effectiveness of the security measures being implemented. This involves
asking the right questions, staying informed about the latest threats,
and holding vendors accountable for their performance. It also requires
executives to ensure that security decisions align with broader business
objectives and that investments in cybersecurity produce real, measurable
results. Cybersecurity must be treated as an integral part of business
strategy, rather than a cost center or burden on innovation.

Rebuilding Trust with Stakeholders

One of the most critical aspects of corporate leadership's role in
cybersecurity is rebuilding trust with stakeholders. Customers,
employees, regulators, and shareholders have all been affected by the
repeated cybersecurity breaches and the revelation of deceptive MFA
claims. To restore trust, corporate leaders must commit to transparency
and accountability in their cybersecurity efforts. This includes openly
communicating about the steps being taken to enhance security,
explaining how these changes will address vulnerabilities, and providing
clear outcomes for stakeholders.

Admitting Past Mistakes

Transparency also requires admitting past mistakes. Corporate leaders
must acknowledge that the previous reliance on public login models
and transmitted data was flawed, and they must explain how their
organizations are correcting those flaws by adopting private access and
digital IDs.

Holding Vendors Accountable

Another critical responsibility for corporate leaders is holding vendors
accountable. Many vendors have profited from selling mitigation products
that merely manage vulnerabilities without fixing them. Leaders must
challenge vendors who continue to push these ineffective strategies and
instead demand real security solutions that address the root cause of
cyber vulnerabilities. By pushing for solutions that offer genuine security,
corporate leaders can signal to stakeholders that they are serious about
making meaningful changes now that the underlying truth has come
to light.

Creating a Culture of Accountability

However, accountability doesn't end with vendors. It must extend
throughout the organization, creating a culture of accountability where
everyone involved in cybersecurity, executives, IT teams, auditors, and
vendors, understand their role in securing the network. Clear expectations
must be set, and performance must be regularly evaluated against those
expectations to ensure continuous improvement to reduce the likelihood
of future breaches.

The Urgency of Leadership Engagement

The complacency of corporate leadership in addressing cybersecurity is
no longer sustainable. The threats are too great, the costs too high, and the
risks too severe. Corporate leaders must lead their organizations toward
genuine security solutions, not just the appearance of compliance. By
doing so, they can protect their organizations from future threats, reduce
legal liabilities, and restore trust with stakeholders.

Conclusion: The Path Forward for Corporate Leadership

The time for passive leadership has passed. The future of cybersecurity requires active engagement from executives who understand the binary nature of security, reject reliance on mitigation strategies that fail to solve the core problem, and rebuild trust by committing to real security solutions. Only by taking ownership of cybersecurity and aligning it with broader business goals can corporate leaders ensure the long-term security and success of their organizations.

CHAPTER 15

The Path to Rebuilding Trust with Vendors and Stakeholders

Acknowledging the Reality

Rebuilding trust in the cybersecurity industry is an essential and difficult task for organizations that have participated in the MFA deception. After years of relying on Single-Factor Authentication (SFA) disguised as Multi-Factor Authentication (MFA) and adding layers of ineffective mitigation, companies now face a stark choice: continue perpetuating the deception or embrace transparency, accountability, and meaningful change to restore credibility and security.

© Christopher Murphy 2025
C. Murphy, *Digital Deception*, Apress Pocket Guides,
https://doi.org/10.1007/979-8-8688-1227-9_15

Admitting Vulnerabilities

The first step in rebuilding trust is acknowledging the reality of the situation. Organizations must recognize that the current reliance on public logins and SFA pretending to be MFA has left their networks exposed to breaches. Denial only deepens the mistrust that exists between organizations and their stakeholders, customers, regulators, and business partners alike. This is not about pointing fingers or assigning blame but about accepting that the security solutions used for decades have proven flawed and that it's time to adopt a new approach and put this chapter behind us.

By admitting these vulnerabilities openly, organizations demonstrate their commitment to rectifying the problem, rather than covering it up. This admission sets the stage for a more open, transparent relationship with stakeholders, where rebuilding trust is based on clear communication and concrete actions. It's a foundational shift from denial to accountability, which is the first step toward mending relationships.

Moving Beyond Mitigation

To rebuild trust, organizations must go beyond surface-level mitigation and adopt real security solutions that address the root cause: public access to secure networks. This means implementing a private access model where digital IDs, combined with genuine MFA, replace public login models and transmitted data, ensuring that user authentication is based on all three required factors, something the user has, something the user knows, and something the user is. The FFIEC regulation the way it was published *is correct*; the steps *will* eliminate the need for guesswork in user identity verification, making the system inherently more secure.

Partnering with Committed Vendors

What's encouraging is that this transition does not have to be disruptive. Organizations can partner with vendors who are committed to real security, moving away from mitigation products and toward solutions that simplify and strengthen their security systems. This shift to genuine MFA compliance demonstrates a tangible commitment to protecting networks and meeting regulatory standards, building trust with all stakeholders.

Embracing Transparency

A major challenge in rebuilding trust is the need for complete transparency. In the past, companies operated under the assumption that they were secure simply because their vendors and auditors certified their compliance. When breaches occurred, it became clear that these assumptions were false, leaving customers, shareholders, and regulators feeling deceived.

Going forward, organizations must commit to a new level of transparency. This means being open about the changes they are making to their security infrastructure, why those changes are necessary, and what outcomes they expect. Stakeholders need to understand how previous vulnerabilities are being addressed and how the organization plans to ensure true security moving forward. Honest communication will build confidence, showing that the company is committed to resolving the underlying problem instead of perpetuating a cycle of mitigation.

Reevaluating Vendor Relationships

For many organizations, rebuilding trust will require reevaluating relationships with vendors. Vendors have long profited from selling SFA disguised as MFA and mitigation products designed to manage vulnerabilities rather than address the root cause of the security flaw. To move forward, companies must challenge these vendors to offer genuine security solutions that prioritize a private access model using digital IDs.

This means holding vendors accountable for the solutions they provide. Organizations may need to cut ties with vendors that continue pushing mitigation-first strategies and instead seek out partners who understand the importance of implementing digital IDs and direct user interaction to secure networks. By aligning with vendors who offer genuine MFA solutions, organizations can signal to stakeholders that they are serious about addressing the security issue at their core.

Acting to Mitigate Risks

Organizations must also realize that delaying action to correct the flaws in their security systems will only increase their legal and reputational risks. As the MFA deception becomes more widely understood, companies that continue to operate under false compliance can face greater scrutiny, class-action lawsuits, regulatory sanctions, and potential public relations crises. The sooner organizations act to address the vulnerability and implement genuine security, the easier it will be to mitigate these risks.

Demonstrating Responsibility

Acting now also demonstrates to stakeholders that the organization is taking responsibility for its role in the global cybersecurity crisis. A proactive approach can help prevent legal exposure and repair relationships with customers and regulators by showing that the company is committed to solving the problem. Waiting only increases the risk of legal exposure, while taking immediate steps to correct the issue can pave the way toward trust recovery.

Creating a Culture of Accountability

Rebuilding trust requires creating a culture of accountability within the organization. Executives must take ownership of the company's cybersecurity strategy and ensure that all team members are aligned with best practices and real security measures. This culture of accountability must also extend to vendors, auditors, and other stakeholders involved in the organization's security infrastructure. By setting clear expectations and holding everyone to higher security standards, organizations can strengthen their cybersecurity posture and foster trust among all stakeholders.

The Path Forward

The path to rebuilding trust is difficult but essential for organizations that want to move beyond the current MFA deception and restore confidence in their security. By admitting the flaw in the current system, adopting real security solutions, and fostering transparency, organizations can repair the damage caused by false compliance and mitigation-first strategies.

Ultimately, the path forward is about more than just improving security; it's about creating a culture of openness, accountability, and genuine commitment to doing the right thing. The future of cybersecurity cannot be built on half-truths and endless patches; it must be rooted in real solutions that address the core problem of public access and weak authentication. Only by embracing these changes can organizations truly rebuild trust with vendors, stakeholders, and the public.

Conclusion: Building a Secure Future

The time for the mitigation model has passed, and the future lies in addressing the root cause of the security vulnerability. For organizations willing to take these steps, the rewards are clear: stronger relationships with stakeholders, reduced legal and financial risks, and a reputation as a leader in cybersecurity accountability. This is the foundation upon which real trust is built, and it's the only way forward for a more secure digital future.

CHAPTER 16

Looking Ahead: The Future of Cybersecurity and he End of the Mitigation Era

Introduction: A Turning Point in Cybersecurity

As we reach the culmination of this journey through the cybersecurity crisis, one thing is clear: the path forward demands a complete departure from the current mitigation-first model. The next era in cybersecurity will be defined by the adoption of a private access model, the implementation of genuine Multi-Factor Authentication (MFA), and the end of reliance on mitigation as a solution. The future lies in preventing breaches through binary security principles rather than simply managing the damage after it occurs.

© Christopher Murphy 2025
C. Murphy, *Digital Deception*, Apress Pocket Guides,
https://doi.org/10.1007/979-8-8688-1227-9_16

The Crossroads of Cybersecurity

The cybersecurity industry is at a crossroads. For years, organizations have relied on mitigation products to protect themselves from cyber threats, adding layers of complexity to an already flawed system. These products have not solved the core problem, public access and guessing identity, but have instead masked it, creating a false sense of security that has left businesses and users vulnerable.

Moving Beyond Mitigation

The next evolution in cybersecurity must focus on eliminating the need for mitigation altogether. By addressing the root cause of the vulnerability, public logins to secure networks, and replacing them with a private access model, we can remove the need for many of the mitigation solutions that are currently in place. This shift will simplify security, reduce costs, and, most importantly, provide real protection for organizations and their users.

CHAPTER 17

The Role of Digital IDs and Direct User Interaction

Introduction: Digital IDs As the Future of Cybersecurity

At the heart of the future of cybersecurity lies the use of digital IDs and direct user interaction. These technologies allow for true MFA, moving away from transmitted data and ensuring that only authorized users can access secure networks. By making private access the default, the need for public logins is eliminated, drastically reducing the surface area for potential attacks.

Transforming Identity Verification

The rise of digital IDs will fundamentally change the way organizations think about identity verification. It will also shift the power balance in cybersecurity, as businesses move from managing identity guessing to

© Christopher Murphy 2025
C. Murphy, *Digital Deception*, Apress Pocket Guides,
https://doi.org/10.1007/979-8-8688-1227-9_17

verifying identity with absolute certainty. This will require an organization-wide commitment to adopting binary security principles, where the system is either secure or not, with no middle ground and no guesswork.

Overcoming Resistance to Change

While the benefits of this shift are clear, the transition will not be without challenges. Understandably, there will be resistance from various sectors of the cybersecurity industry, particularly from those who have built their business models around mitigation. These companies may resist change, as the adoption of a private access model and digital IDs could render many of their products and services obsolete.

Similarly, corporate leaders may hesitate to embrace the change, fearing the perceived costs or disruptions associated with implementing new security solutions. However, as discussed throughout this book, the cost of inaction, both in terms of financial losses and legal exposure, is far greater than the cost of adopting a real security solution. The key to overcoming this resistance is education and awareness, showing leaders that the transition to private access can be seamless, cost-effective, and ultimately beneficial for the long-term success of their organizations.

Simplifying Cybersecurity

The opportunity for the cybersecurity industry to evolve is immense. By focusing on simplification rather than complexity, the industry can move away from the illusion that more layers of mitigation equal more security. Instead, the future will be built on the understanding that less is more, fewer layers, fewer points of failure, and fewer opportunities for attackers to exploit.

Benefits for Organizations

The adoption of a private access model and genuine MFA will allow organizations to strip away the unnecessary mitigation products that have dominated the market. This will not only reduce operational costs but also make networks inherently more secure. The constant patching and updating will diminish, allowing businesses to focus on growth rather than constantly reacting to the latest threats.

Benefits for Users

Users will also benefit from a more secure Internet. With digital IDs and private access, their personal information will be better protected, and they will no longer be victims of the MFA deception that has left them exposed to cybercrime. This shift will restore trust in online security, giving users confidence that their data is truly safe.

Rebuilding Trust Through Real Security

The erosion of trust between companies and their users has been a defining feature of the cybersecurity crisis. Every breach, every false promise of MFA compliance, and every instance of identity theft has chipped away at the belief that companies can protect the personal information entrusted to them. As companies adopt real security measures, such as digital IDs and private access, they have the opportunity to rebuild trust by demonstrating that they are no longer relying on inadequate security models.

The Need for Action

The future of cybersecurity is clear, but it requires action. The mitigation era must end, and the industry must embrace a real security solution that solves the root cause of the vulnerability. Corporate leaders, vendors, and regulators must work together to implement a private access model and digital IDs that provide genuine MFA.

A Cultural and Technological Shift

This shift is not just technological, it's cultural. It requires a commitment to binary security, where systems are either secure or they are not. The era of guessing identity and relying on transmitted data is over. The next generation of cybersecurity will be built on certainty, providing a safer, more secure Internet for everyone.

The Path to a Secure Future

The path to a secure future is not without its challenges; however, the rewards are immense. By embracing a private access model, adopting digital IDs, and moving away from mitigation, the cybersecurity industry can finally address the root cause of the security vulnerability. This will lead to a simpler, more secure world where cybercrime is no longer an inevitable consequence of doing business online.

Conclusion: Embracing Lasting Change

Now is the time to bring about lasting change. The cybersecurity industry must rise to the challenge, they must take responsibility for the failures of the past, and together we must build a future where security is no longer an afterthought but a foundational principle. Corporate leaders must prioritize genuine security solutions and stop relying on mitigation strategies that only address symptoms. By embracing private access and digital IDs, organizations can once and for all eliminate the need for identity guessing and public logins, creating a safer environment for businesses and users alike.

Prevention over Mitigation

In this new era, cybersecurity will be about prevention, not mitigation. It will be about protecting systems before breaches happen, rather than scrambling to manage the damage afterward. The end of the mitigation era is in sight, and the path forward is crystal clear. The future of cybersecurity lies in simplicity, certainty, and a commitment to a real solution that secures the digital world for generations to come.

A Vision for the Future

The journey may be long, but the destination is worth the effort, a secure Internet, built on trust and binary security principles, where cybercrime is no longer a threat and users can confidently engage in the digital world. This is the future of cybersecurity, and the time to embrace it is now.

CHAPTER 18

A Call for Integrity and Real Security

Introduction: Exposing the Cybersecurity Crisis

Our journey through the cybersecurity crisis has exposed the false sense of security that has dominated the industry for decades. The decision to embrace public access models, combined with the deception surrounding Multi-Factor Authentication (MFA), has led to a world where breaches are inevitable, mitigation solutions are relied upon, and real security has been sacrificed in favor of convenience. But the time for accepting mitigation and false compliance has passed.

The Binary Truth of Security

At its foundation, computer science and cybersecurity are built on binary logic. Systems are either secure, or they are not. There is no gray area, no room for guesswork. Yet, the current state of cybersecurity has relied on transmitted data and public access models, both of which inherently introduce vulnerabilities. The core problem is not the complexity of cyber threats but the failure to follow the binary truth of security.

© Christopher Murphy 2025
C. Murphy, *Digital Deception*, Apress Pocket Guides,
https://doi.org/10.1007/979-8-8688-1227-9_18

The Root Cause: Public Access Models

This book has argued that the decision to grant public access to secure networks set the stage for today's cybercrime crisis. By relying on identity guessing through transmitted data, organizations opened the door to breaches and have since spent billions of dollars trying to mitigate the consequences. But mitigation was never the answer. The only solution is to correct the original error and adopt a private access model and digital IDs that provide genuine MFA.

The Failure of Mitigation-First Approaches

As explored in detail, the mitigation-first approach has dominated cybersecurity for far too long. Companies, vendors, and auditors have built entire industries around managing vulnerabilities rather than addressing the root cause. This has led to a tangled web of security products that do little more than mask the problem, all while expanding the attack surface.

The Cost of Complacency

The cost of continuing down this path is too great, not only financially but in terms of trust, security, and integrity. The mitigation model must be abandoned in favor of real security solutions that eliminate the need for layers of patchwork. This shift requires a fundamental change in the way organizations think about security: it is not about adding more layers but about setting the foundation straight.

The Solution: Private Access Models and Digital IDs

The solution to the cybersecurity crisis lies in the adoption of a private access model and digital IDs. This approach eliminates the reliance on public logins and transmitted data, replacing them with binary verification, either the user has the digital ID and is authorized, or they do not. By combining digital IDs with direct user interaction, the system becomes inherently secure and meets the true requirements of MFA.

A Practical Solution for Today

This is not a distant vision for the future; it is a practical, proven solution that can be implemented today. By making private access the default and eliminating the need for public access, organizations can drastically reduce the risk of breaches and create a simpler, more secure system. The technology exists, and the only thing standing in the way is the willingness to embrace it.

The Role of Corporate Leadership

Throughout this book, we have emphasized the role of corporate leadership in securing their organizations. Leaders can no longer afford to delegate security to vendors and IT departments without oversight. They must take direct responsibility for the cybersecurity strategy, ensuring that real solutions are implemented and that mitigation is no longer seen as an acceptable answer.

Rejecting False Promises

This requires corporate leaders to reject the false promises of vendors who sell mitigation products and instead demand real security solutions, ones that address the root problem of public access and Single-Factor Authentication (SFA) masquerading as MFA. By aligning cybersecurity with the broader business goals of the organization, leaders can create a security culture built on integrity, transparency, and strength.

Rebuilding Trust in the Industry

The cybersecurity industry has suffered from a breakdown of trust, largely due to the false claims of MFA compliance and the widespread use of mitigation-first strategies. Vendors and auditors have been complicit in perpetuating this deception, and now they must take responsibility for their role in the crisis.

Accountability for Vendors and Auditors

To rebuild trust, vendors must start offering a real security solution that provides private access and genuine MFA. Auditors, too, must hold organizations accountable and refuse to certify systems that do not meet the true standards of MFA in the spirit of which the authors of the FFIEC regulations were intended. The future of cybersecurity depends on honesty, integrity, and a commitment to binary security principles.

A Call to Action

The cybersecurity crisis was not inevitable, but it is the result of choices made over decades. Now, we stand at a critical juncture. The industry must decide whether to continue down the path of mitigation and false compliance or embrace the truth and adopt real solutions.

The Ultimate Solution: Integrity

The call to action is clear: organizations must adopt a private access model and digital IDs, corporate leaders must take direct responsibility for their cybersecurity strategy, and vendors must stop selling products that perpetuate the deception. The mitigation era must come to an end, and the future must be built on real security.

Conclusion: Building a Secure Future

The ultimate solution to the cybersecurity crisis is integrity. Corporate leaders, vendors, and auditors must be willing to confront the uncomfortable truth that the current system is flawed and that public access models and SFA masquerading as MFA cannot provide real security. The answer lies in binary security principles, where systems are either secure or not and where mitigation is no longer seen as an acceptable substitute for real protection.

The future of cybersecurity belongs to those who are willing to embrace the truth and make the necessary changes to secure their networks. It is only through this commitment to integrity and action that we can build a safer, more secure world.

This book is a call for integrity, for real security solutions that go beyond the surface and address the root cause of the vulnerability. The time for mitigation and false promises is over. The future of cybersecurity depends on our willingness to embrace real change, to adopt a private access model, and to ensure that every system is secure.

The choice is clear: continue down the path of false security or take the bold step toward true protection. The future of cybersecurity is in our hands, and it is up to us to make it secure.

CHAPTER 19

The Impact of AI on Cybersecurity

Introduction: Opportunities and Challenges of AI

The rise of artificial intelligence (AI) in cybersecurity has introduced both significant opportunities and profound challenges. On one hand, AI's capacity to process massive amounts of data, identify patterns, and automate responses promises to enhance security measures in ways previously unimaginable. On the other hand, AI's integration into a cybersecurity framework built on the flawed foundation of public access presents new vulnerabilities that could escalate the already intense battle between cyber defenders and attackers.

The Potential of AI in Cybersecurity

AI's potential in cybersecurity is undeniable. It can analyze vast datasets at speeds unattainable by human analysts, enabling real-time detection and response to threats. AI-driven tools have the potential to transform the cybersecurity landscape, offering more accurate and faster identification

© Christopher Murphy 2025
C. Murphy, *Digital Deception*, Apress Pocket Guides,
https://doi.org/10.1007/979-8-8688-1227-9_19

of threats, automating routine tasks, and even predicting potential attacks before they occur. These tools are designed to learn and adapt, making them invaluable in a rapidly evolving threat landscape.

The Dual-Edged Nature of AI

However, this power cuts both ways. Just as defenders can leverage AI, so too can attackers. Cybercriminals are increasingly using AI to develop more sophisticated attacks, automate phishing campaigns, and evade detection by traditional security measures. The battlefield is no longer merely between human defenders and attackers; it is now AI versus AI, with both sides deploying advanced algorithms to outmaneuver the other. This AI arms race is a supercharged version of the perpetual cat-and-mouse game that has characterized cybersecurity since the introduction of public access to secure networks.

Weaponization of AI by Cybercriminals

Recent reports have highlighted how AI is being weaponized by cybercriminals. For example, AI-driven attacks are increasingly being used to mimic human behavior, making phishing campaigns and social engineering tactics more convincing than ever before. AI algorithms can analyze vast amounts of publicly available information, such as social media profiles, to craft personalized and highly effective phishing emails. These AI-enhanced attacks not only increase the likelihood of success but also reduce the time and effort required for cybercriminals to launch them.

The Foundational Flaw in AI-Based Security

The problem with AI in network security, however, stems not from the technology itself but from the foundational flaw on which it is built. Again, the introduction of public access to secure networks, a decision made decades ago, created a fundamental weakness that no amount of AI or other security measures can fully address on this path. The endless loop of patching breaches, hoping the fix is sufficient, and then reacting to the next exploit has defined cybersecurity for years. AI, despite its power, is still layered onto this flawed system, making it a participant in this cycle rather than a solution.

AI's Limitations in Addressing Public Access Models

AI can enhance the capabilities of cybersecurity, but it cannot rectify the core issue: the reliance on public access models. So long as public logins remain the gateway to secure networks, AI will be fighting a battle it cannot win. Attackers will continue to exploit this fundamental weakness, using AI to develop ever more sophisticated methods to breach defenses.

The Rush to Adopt AI Without Understanding

The introduction of AI into cybersecurity is emblematic of a broader issue that has plagued the industry for decades: the rush to adopt new technologies without fully understanding their implications. Time and again, cybersecurity measures have been introduced with an attitude of "look what we can do," without sufficient consideration of "should we do it?" AI, like every other technological advancement in the field, is being

applied long before its full impact is known or understood. This haste
has led to the creation of an even more complex and fragile security
environment, where each new tool adds another layer of potential failure.

Digital ID Technology: A Solution Beyond AI

Yet, there is a solution that AI cannot overcome, a security measure that
stands outside the reach of even the most advanced AI-driven attacks:
digital ID technology. Once public logins are closed, and uniquely
serialized, encrypted digital IDs are deployed, the game changes entirely.
AI, no matter how advanced, cannot physically connect a digital ID with
a one-to-one relationship to a system. This shift from public to private
access transforms the security landscape, moving the battlefield from the
realm of guesswork and transmitted data to one of binary certainty.

The Power of Digital ID Technology

Digital ID technology introduces a level of security that AI alone *cannot*
achieve. By ensuring that only users with a properly configured, uniquely
serialized, and physically connected digital ID can access a network,
organizations can eliminate the vulnerabilities introduced by public
access. This is a security feature that AI, on either side of the equation,
cannot impersonate or bypass.

Breaking the Endless Cycle of Mitigation

Without this shift to digital ID technology, the future of network security
looks bleak, even with the most sophisticated AI tools at our disposal. AI's
role in cybersecurity, as it stands, is to perpetuate the ongoing struggle
between defenders and attackers, a struggle that is exacerbated by the

flawed foundation of public access. The history of cybersecurity has been one of patching breaches, praying that the fix holds, and then repeating the process with each new exploit.

The Core Problem: Identity Guessing

Yet, there is a deeper issue at play, one that AI cannot solve. The endless loop of guessing identity, where AI is used to both defend against and execute identity-based attacks, represents the core of the problem. As AI becomes more adept at mimicking human behavior, the distinction between legitimate and illegitimate users becomes increasingly blurred. This is where the current model of network security, built on public access and identity guessing, will ultimately collapse.

Transforming Security with Digital IDs

With the integration of digital ID technology, however, this cycle can be broken. AI can then be used not to fight a losing battle but to enhance a fundamentally secure system. The deployment of digital IDs ensures that the most crucial aspect of security, proof of identity and presence, is beyond the reach of AI-driven attacks. It creates a binary decision-making process where the system is either secure because the digital ID is present or it is not because it isn't.

AI's Role in a Secure Future

The integration of AI into cybersecurity presents significant opportunities, but its effectiveness is ultimately undermined by the flawed foundation of public access models. The future of network security does not lie in continuing the endless cycle of mitigation but in embracing a shift to private access through digital ID technology. AI will undoubtedly play a critical role in this future, but it must be part of a broader strategy that addresses the root cause of security vulnerabilities.

Building a Binary Security Environment

By adopting digital ID technology and closing the door on public access, organizations can confidently create a security environment where AI enhances protection rather than simply fighting to keep up with the latest threats. This shift is not just a technological necessity; it is a fundamental rethinking of what true cybersecurity means in an age where AI is both the defender and the attacker. The future of cybersecurity will be defined not by the complexity of the solutions we layer onto a flawed system but by the simplicity and certainty of binary security principles.

Conclusion: AI and the Future of Cybersecurity

In the end, the question is not just about what AI can do in the realm of cybersecurity but what it should do. Without careful consideration and the right foundational security measures, AI could very well accelerate the very problems it was designed to solve. The path forward must be one of careful, thoughtful application, where technology is applied in a manner that aligns with the fundamental principles of security, rather than merely showcasing the next big thing.

Stephen Hawking's biggest warning is about the rise of artificial intelligence: "It will either be the best thing that's ever happened to us, or it will be the worst thing. If we're not careful, it very well may be the last thing."

Do you want to play a game?

—The movie *WarGames*

CHAPTER 20

The Global Landscape: Cybersecurity Challenges Across Borders

Introduction: A Connected World and Its Challenges

The rise of the Internet has connected the world like never before, creating a global marketplace for information, commerce, and communication. However, this interconnectedness has also introduced significant cybersecurity challenges that transcend national borders. As cyber threats become increasingly sophisticated and widespread, the lack of a unified global approach to cybersecurity has left organizations and individuals vulnerable to cross-border attacks.

© Christopher Murphy 2025
C. Murphy, *Digital Deception*, Apress Pocket Guides,
https://doi.org/10.1007/979-8-8688-1227-9_20

Regulatory Frameworks Across Borders

One of the most significant challenges in global cybersecurity is the variation in regulatory frameworks across different countries. While some nations have implemented stringent cybersecurity laws and regulations, others have lagged, creating a patchwork of standards that are difficult to navigate and enforce.

For example, the European Union's General Data Protection Regulation (GDPR) has set a high standard for data protection, with strict requirements for how organizations collect, store, and use personal data. In contrast, the United States has taken a more sectoral approach, with different regulations for different industries, such as the Health Insurance Portability and Accountability Act (HIPAA) for healthcare and the Gramm-Leach-Bliley Act (GLBA) for financial institutions.

The Complexity of Cross-Border Compliance

These regulatory differences can create challenges for multinational organizations that must comply with a myriad of laws and regulations in the countries where they operate. Compliance becomes even more complex when data crosses borders, as it may be subject to the laws of multiple jurisdictions. This can lead to conflicts between regulatory requirements, making it difficult for organizations to ensure they are fully compliant while also maintaining robust cybersecurity practices.

Safe Havens for Cybercriminals

In addition, the lack of a unified global approach to cybersecurity has allowed cybercriminals to exploit regulatory gaps. Countries with weaker cybersecurity laws or enforcement can become safe havens for cybercriminals, who can launch attacks on organizations in countries with stronger protections, knowing that they are less likely to face prosecution.

The Borderless Nature of Cybercrime

The borderless nature of the Internet has made it easier for cybercriminals to operate across jurisdictions, often with little fear of being caught or prosecuted. Cross-border cybercrime can take many forms, from ransomware attacks and data breaches to intellectual property theft and espionage.

Challenges in Prosecution and Cooperation

One of the challenges in combating cross-border cybercrime is the difficulty in tracking down and prosecuting perpetrators. Cybercriminals can operate from anywhere in the world, often using tools and techniques that make it difficult to trace their activities back to a specific location. Even when law enforcement agencies can identify the source of an attack, bringing the perpetrators to justice can be challenging due to differences in legal systems, extradition treaties, and the willingness of countries to cooperate in cybercrime investigations.

The Far-Reaching Consequences of Cybercrime

The global nature of cybercrime also means that the consequences of an attack can be far-reaching. A data breach in one country can have implications for individuals and organizations around the world, particularly when the compromised data includes personal information or intellectual property. In addition, cross-border cyberattacks can strain diplomatic relations between countries, particularly when state-sponsored actors are involved.

The Need for International Cooperation

Addressing the challenges of cross-border cybercrime requires international cooperation. Countries must work together to develop and enforce global cybersecurity standards, share threat intelligence, and collaborate on investigations and prosecutions.

Efforts by International Organizations

Organizations like the United Nations and the European Union have made efforts to promote international cooperation on cybersecurity, but much work remains to be done. The Budapest Convention on Cybercrime, for example, is the only legally binding international treaty on cybercrime, and while it has been ratified by many countries, some key players, including Russia, North Korea, and China, have not signed on.

Bilateral and Multilateral Agreements

In addition to international treaties, bilateral and multilateral agreements between countries can play a crucial role in enhancing cybersecurity cooperation. For example, the United States has signed cybersecurity agreements with countries like Japan, Israel, and the United Kingdom, which include provisions for information sharing, joint investigations, and capacity building.

The Role of the Private Sector

Private sector companies also have a role to play in fostering international cooperation on cybersecurity. Multinational corporations in particular are well-positioned to share best practices and collaborate with governments and other organizations to enhance global cybersecurity. By working together, public and private sector entities can help close the gaps in cybersecurity protections and make it more difficult for cybercriminals to operate across borders.

Preparing for the Future of Cybercrime

The challenges of cross-border cybercrime are likely to grow as the Internet continues to evolve and more devices become connected. To address these challenges, the global community must prioritize cybersecurity as a critical issue that requires coordinated action. This will involve not only strengthening existing laws and regulations but also developing new frameworks that can adapt to the changing landscape of cyber threats.

Building Trust and Cooperation

The future of global cybersecurity will also depend on the ability of countries to build trust and cooperate with one another. This will require overcoming geopolitical tensions and finding common ground on issues like data protection, encryption, and the role of state actors in cyberspace.

Conclusion: A Unified Approach to Cybersecurity

As cyber threats continue to evolve, so too must the strategies used to combat them. The next era of cybersecurity will be defined by the ability of the global community to come together and develop a unified approach to protecting the Internet and the people who rely on it.

CHAPTER 21

A New Era of Network Security Through Real Computer Science

Reflecting on the State of Cybersecurity

As we reflect on the journey we've taken through the chapters of this book, it's clear that the state of cybersecurity today is not the result of one failure but rather the accumulation of thousands of compromises, each chipping away at the integrity of our digital world. The cost of these compromises is measured not only in economic terms but in the erosion of trust, the undermining of legal standards, and the perpetuation of global deception that has affected each and every user of the Internet and beyond.

Identifying the Foundational Flaws

The chapters of this book have meticulously laid out the foundational flaw in our current approach to cybersecurity: the original sin of public access, the widespread deception of Multi-Factor Authentication, the complicity of the education systems, the failures of regulation, and the blind

© Christopher Murphy 2025
C. Murphy, *Digital Deception*, Apress Pocket Guides,
https://doi.org/10.1007/979-8-8688-1227-9_21

conformity that has allowed this crisis to fester and grow exponentially. We have also seen how the victims, every Internet user, every business, every institution, bear the brunt of these failures, while those who profit from the status quo continue to do so without accountability.

A Story of Hope and Binary Truths

Yet, this is not a story without hope. The facts we've presented, the binary truths that computer science offers, give us a clear path forward. The solution is elegantly simple, rooted in the very principles that have been ignored for far too long. By embracing a unified model of security, grounded in real computer science and direct user interaction through digital IDs, we can restore control to the networks, eliminate the vulnerabilities of public logins, and finally put an end to the era of mitigation.

A Call for Integrity and Leadership

This is not merely a technical challenge; it is a call for integrity, for leadership, and for a collective commitment to rebuild what has been lost. The tools we need are already at our disposal; the science is absolute. What remains is the willingness to act, to reject the flawed systems that have brought us here, and to embrace the real, verifiable security that can protect us in the digital age.

Turning the Tide with Real Computer Science

Together, we have the power to turn the tide. By applying real computer science to meet the security requirements of the Internet, we can create a future where trust is restored, where the economy is protected, and where the Internet is a place of safety and innovation rather than a crime scene. It is time to end the era of convenience over security and to begin the era of real solutions, solutions that are as simple as they are effective, as binary as they are absolute.

Conclusion: The Case for Change

The chapters of this book make the case for change. Now, it is up to us, together, to make that change a reality. The path forward is clear, the science is sound, and the future is in our hands. Let us step into it with the confidence that we can and will build a safer, more secure digital world.

I now invite the community to read *Quantum Security*, to fully grasp the full power of private access and digital IDs. Once public logins are closed and uniquely serialized, encrypted digital IDs are deployed, the world will come to know the full potential of the Internet.

Glossary

AI (Artificial Intelligence)

The simulation of human intelligence in machines programmed to think, learn, and adapt. Often leveraged in cybersecurity for threat detection and automation but also exploited by attackers.

Binary Security

A concept emphasizing absolute security, where systems are either secure or insecure with no gray areas.

CTA (Cyber Threat Alliance)

An industry collaboration sharing threat intelligence to enhance global cybersecurity efforts.

Cybercrime Ecosystem

The interconnected network of malicious actors, tools, and systems enabling global cyberattacks.

Data-Sharing Agreements

Formal arrangements between entities or nations to exchange threat intelligence and enhance collective cybersecurity.

Deepfake

AI-generated media, such as audio or video, manipulated to impersonate individuals for malicious purposes.

Digital ID (Digital Identification)

A secure, encrypted form of identity verification ensuring direct user authentication without transmitted credentials.

FFIEC (Federal Financial Institutions Examination Council)

A US interagency body prescribing uniform principles for financial institutions, including cybersecurity standards.

© Christopher Murphy 2025
C. Murphy, *Digital Deception*, Apress Pocket Guides,
https://doi.org/10.1007/979-8-8688-1227-9

GDPR (General Data Protection Regulation)
A regulation enacted by the European Union to protect personal data and privacy, imposing strict requirements on organizations handling EU citizens' data.

GLBA (Gramm-Leach-Bliley Act)
A US regulation mandating financial institutions to protect customers' private information.

HIPAA (Health Insurance Portability and Accountability Act)
A US legislation providing data privacy and security provisions for safeguarding medical information.

Identity Guessing
A vulnerability arising from systems relying on transmitted data to infer user identity rather than verifying it directly.

MFA (Multi-Factor Authentication)
A security system requiring multiple forms of identification to verify a user's identity. True MFA involves distinct factors: something the user knows, has, and is.

Mitigation Model
An approach to cybersecurity that layers defenses on existing systems instead of addressing foundational vulnerabilities.

Patch and Pray
A colloquial term describing reliance on mitigation strategies that temporarily address vulnerabilities without solving root causes.

Private Access Model
A cybersecurity framework replacing public logins with direct, secure user authentication via digital IDs.

Serialized Encryption
A method of encrypting and uniquely identifying digital IDs to prevent unauthorized access.

SFA (Single-Factor Authentication)

A less secure authentication method relying on a single form of identity verification, such as a password. Often misrepresented as MFA.

VPN (Virtual Private Network)

A secure connection method creating a private connection over a public network, often used to protect data transmissions.

GPSR Compliance
The European Union's (EU) General Product Safety Regulation (GPSR) is a set
of rules that requires consumer products to be safe and our obligations to
ensure this.

If you have any concerns about our products, you can contact us on

ProductSafety@springernature.com

In case Publisher is established outside the EU, the EU authorized
representative is:

Springer Nature Customer Service Center GmbH
Europaplatz 3
69115 Heidelberg, Germany